MOSCOW

By Leo Gruliow
and the Editors of Time-Life Books

With photographs by Pete Turner
and Dick Rowan

THE GREAT CITIES · TIME-LIFE BOOKS · AMSTERDAM

The Author: Leo Gruliow is an American journalist and specialist on Soviet affairs. He founded and for more than 25 years ran *The Current Digest of The Soviet Press*, a weekly published at the Ohio State University. He first went to Moscow, as a journalist, in 1933 and stayed almost five years. During the Second World War he returned as representative for U.S. Russian War Relief and was awarded the Soviet Distinguished Labour Medal for his work in aid of Soviet civilians. He went back as a visitor in the late 1950s and again from 1972 to 1975 as a correspondent, first for the *Christian Science Monitor* and then for the *Saturday Evening Post*.

The Photographers: A graduate of the Rochester Institute of Technology, Pete Turner has had his photographs for both editorial and advertising media published internationally. One-man exhibitions of his work have been held in Europe and the United States. He is also represented in the permanent collection of the International Museum of Photography at George Eastman House, Rochester, New York.

Dick Rowan began his career as a news photographer covering Adlai Stevenson's 1956 campaign for the Presidency of the United States. Shortly thereafter he was employed by LIFE Magazine's photographer studio, and ultimately became a successful freelance photojournalist.

TIME
LIFE
BOOKS

THE WORLD'S WILD PLACES
HUMAN BEHAVIOUR
THE ART OF SEWING
THE OLD WEST
THE EMERGENCE OF MAN
LIFE LIBRARY OF PHOTOGRAPHY
TIME-LIFE LIBRARY OF ART
FOODS OF THE WORLD
GREAT AGES OF MAN
LIFE SCIENCE LIBRARY
LIFE NATURE LIBRARY

EDITOR: Dale Brown
Design Consultant: Louis Klein
Picture Editor: Pamela Marke
Assistant Picture Editor: Anne Angus

Editorial Staff for Moscow:
Deputy Editor: Windsor Chorlton
Designer: Roy Williams
Staff Writers: Mike Brown, Jim Hicks, Deborah Thompson
Picture Researcher: Gunn Brinson
Text Researchers: Susie Dawson, Vanessa Kramer
Design Assistant: Shirin Patel

Editorial Production for the Series
Art Department: Julia West
Editorial Department: Ellen Brush, Jan Piggott, Betty H. Weatherley
Picture Department: Thelma Gilbert, Christine Hinze

The captions and the text of the picture essays were written by the staff of TIME-LIFE Books.

Valuable assistance in the preparation of this volume was given by Agnes Forrest Gruliow, London, Ohio, and Felix Rosenthal, TIME Bureau, Moscow.

Published by TIME-LIFE International (Nederland) B.V.
Ottho Heldrinstraat 5, Amsterdam 1018.

Cover: Red stars—celestial symbols of the Soviet state—glow on the Kremlin's ancient towers under a full moon.

Last end paper: A swarm of white-limbed Muscovites, taking advantage of a hot summer day, sprawl on a grassy bank in Gorky Park, the most popular of Moscow's many open spaces.

First end paper: Twin doves and flowers decorate part of a stained-glass panel in the Novoslobodskaya Metro Station.

Contents

I

A View behind the Curtain

Moscow has existed since the middle of the 12th Century, and most of the foreigners who visit it go there to view the splendours of its past. But today's Moscow—the Moscow of the Muscovites—is a new city that spreads out in concentric rings from the medieval core.

This new city has shot up in a single century. Most of old Moscow disappeared in flames during the 39-day occupation by Napoleon's Grande Armée in 1812. The great fire destroyed more than two-thirds of that "Asiatic city of countless churches, Moscow the holy," as Tolstoy called the "mother city" in *War and Peace.* Although Moscow was soon rebuilt, it remained a muddy, sprawling town—an overgrown village, the aristocrats of St. Petersburg called it. Not until the emancipation of the serfs in 1861 did it begin its steady rise. That was when peasants poured in from the countryside to man new mills and factories. The city became the country's rail hub. It went on growing in spite of wars, revolution and famine. It is still growing. Traffic rushes down 12-lane avenues. Wrecking crews are ripping out rows of buildings to carve additional boulevards across the city. Building cranes stand against the sky everywhere: one day I counted 88 within a single mile. Construction plans run to the year 2000. Meanwhile the city remains raw and unfinished.

Approaching Moscow from any direction is a surprise. One moment you are in the gently rolling countryside, spinning past fields and woods. Tipsy, log cottages, their window frames trimmed with elaborate fretwork, dot the roadside. They are redolent of old Russia and they stir your imagination. You anticipate historic Moscow: St. Basil's peppermint-stick domes, the red-brick Kremlin walls, the golden cupolas of the cathedrals and monasteries. But the next moment thick clusters of apartment houses loom, 16, 18, 22 storeys high, half of the buildings unfinished and topped by cranes. The transition from country to city is abrupt. As Moscow has grown, it has swallowed up outlying towns and villages. Its rim is an advancing wall of tall, white concrete buildings.

The scale of the construction, the pace of change, can surprise even a New Yorker like myself, used to the sight of his hometown being torn down and built up again—but in New York I take such development for granted. Here the new buildings impress me, and for a very good reason. I know what it took to build them. As an American newspaperman, I have had an advantage denied most other foreigners who have only visited the Soviet Union: I have lived in Moscow off and on over a span of 40 years and have seen it grow from a turbulent city of three million inhabitants,

The urban sprawl of modern Moscow beyond the window serves as a backdrop to a hotel room whose décor—the patterned lace curtain and mushroom table lamp—is redolent of the 1930s. Although much of Moscow has been built since the Second World War, the interiors of many of the city's buildings still have a dated look by Western standards.

still marked by traces of revolution and civil war, to today's ambitious metropolis of seven and a half million.

I first saw Moscow in the 1930s when its people were caught up in one of the most sweeping programmes of industrialization the world had seen. I spent more than four years there then. I returned in 1943 for another two years, shortly after the Muscovites had beaten off Hitler's armies from their gates. I visited it again in the late 1950s, during the Cold War. And I returned in the early '70s, there to live in one of those postwar apartment buildings with my wife and daughter for another three years. Each time I found a different city, a new Moscow. It is still changing.

I know that today's frantic construction is simply a rush to catch up with overdue needs; I know that, when I enter these tall buildings, the signs of the haste with which they were put together dismay me. Yet the sight of them still stirs me, for I know what they mean to the people who built them and who call them home.

I propose, therefore, to tell the story of Moscow in terms of my own experience—to reveal it to you a decade at a time, starting with the 1930s, before examining its historic past, its present and its future.

Bundled up in wool and fur, Muscovites surge up and down the staircase leading to a Metro station. The most efficient transport system in Moscow, the Metro carries about five million people a day—more than any other subway system in the world—on its 100 miles of track.

I came to Moscow in 1933, when a whole generation of correspondents was reporting on the growing pains of the young Soviet state. The Civil War had been over for little more than ten years, but already change was sweeping the city. The Soviet Union—largely peopled by peasants, the majority only newly literate—had set out by decree to catch up with the Western industrial powers in one decade. It had reorganized its strip farms into huge collectives and in 1928 had embarked on the first of a series of five-year plans—massive programmes of industrialization. Uprooted peasants poured into Moscow to work in the new factories. The city's population had grown by a million in the space of three years. Moscow was bursting at the seams.

To a romantic, footloose young journalist, revolutionary Moscow was a magnet; but I got there only by chance. I had lost my job on an American newspaper during the Depression and, when I heard that the Russians were starting an English-language daily newspaper aimed at the many foreign engineers who had been hired to set up factories, I applied for a job as make-up man, and got it. I did not know quite what to expect of Moscow. My parents were Russian-born, but they had emigrated from St. Petersburg at the turn of the century. I knew very little about the country of my ancestors, and I could speak no Russian.

I sailed from London to Leningrad, the old St. Petersburg, and travelled on to Moscow by train. In those days the First Class compartments had plush seats and heavy sliding doors; I rode Third Class, well-named "hard", for the compartments had plank seats covered with thin pallets for bedding, and no doors. At night, as we swayed and rattled across the flat

northern plain, dim electric bulbs mounted in the old brass lanterns cast a feeble yellow light in the corridors.

We reached Moscow in the early morning. I walked along the station platform and entered a cavernous waiting room packed with humanity—like a Breughel painting in monochrome. Grizzled peasants and kerchiefed women filled the rows of benches; others sat on luggage in the aisles or slept on their bundles. Several mothers were nursing babies. A smell of sweat, disinfectant and the peasants' strong tobacco—*makhorka*, smoked in a twist of newspaper—filled the room.

The scene was reminiscent of Ellis Island, America's disembarkation point for immigrants like my parents in the late 19th and early 20th Centuries. In a way it was an Ellis Island. The first five-year plan had just ended, the second was just beginning. Russia had still not recovered from the turmoil of collectivization: bewildered peasants were streaming into the cities by the thousands. Moscow was both a crossroads and the focal point of this mass migration.

The street outside the station was also jammed with a steady stream of human traffic. Passengers with cardboard or wicker suitcases, wooden trunks and luggage sewn into protective cloth covers were pouring out of the station; some carried their possessions in sacks slung over their shoulders. They parted to make way for a group of young men and women marching raggedly behind a banner and singing. One young man bellowed out the verses, the others took up the refrain. As the street crowd closed behind them, I wondered who the marchers were. Students, mobilized to help gather in the harvest, or off on an excursion? Workers, leaving for jobs at one of the new dams or other industrial projects? I could only guess.

Wooden trams, trains of three cars hitched together in tandem, rattled noisily through the cobbled square. Bells clanged a warning as pedestrians darted across the tracks in front of them. At the tram-stop, passengers swarmed aboard; those who could not squeeze inside clung like clusters of bees on the steps of the moving vehicles.

A Moscow guide, sent by the newspaper, met me at the station. As we took our places in a line to wait for a taxi, he pointed out a wooden barrier from behind which came the din of pneumatic drills: Moscow's new underground system, he said proudly, the Metro. It would be some years before that efficient transport system came into operation; now it was difficult even to find a taxi. After a fruitless wait, my guide hailed a *droshky*, one of the last of those antiquated, horse-drawn open carriages. He bargained with the bearded, surly coachman and we clambered in. As I took my seat, dust rose from the worn padding. The nag started up, hoofs clattering on the cobbles, and went jogging down a narrow street that led off the square.

From my perch in the *droshky*, the crowd was reduced to a bobbing sea of kerchiefs and caps. Wherever the pavement narrowed, the pedestrians spilled on to the road. I spotted villagers shuffling along in belted smocks

Moscow's old architectural treasures no longer stand supreme against the open sky as they did in 1860 (inset). Now, huge modern buildings dwarf the Kremlin's cathedrals, while the giant Rossia Hotel (right foreground) almost hides St. Basil's Cathedral and the Spassky Tower. But even the hotel's overwhelming bulk cannot subdue little St. Anne's Church, standing defiantly before it as a reminder of the past.

and, here and there, a leather-coated manager or bureaucrat striding along purposefully, swinging a briefcase. Some of the pedestrians ambled down the middle of the road as heedlessly as if it were a country lane.

Between breaks in the crowd I glimpsed shop windows. They were bare except for posters portraying Red Army soldiers in greatcoats, or brawny workers with upraised hammers. On a few streets loudspeakers, mounted on lamp posts, blared martial tunes. Everywhere there were signs of construction. Many of the buildings were encased in scaffolding, some were boarded up. Workmen were mixing mortar in large wooden troughs on the pavements, others carried loads of bricks stacked higgledy-piggledy on two-man barrows. Many of the workers were women, dressed in black smocks and black kerchiefs. Occasionally, trucks loaded with building materials passed the *droshky*, honking.

Later that day I tried to add up my impressions. I had spent a few days in Leningrad *en route*, and now I compared Moscow to the former capital. Leningrad was a stately European city, and even where it was run down it preserved an air of elegance; but Moscow was burly and rough. Vaguely it reminded me of something, and suddenly I knew—an American boom town of the 19th Century.

On the days that followed I explored the city. The bustle contrasted with Moscow's curiously old-fashioned air. The log houses that I saw tucked away among the taller brick buildings did not seem inappropriate, however: somehow they reinforced my image of a frontier town. It was the 19th-Century mansions with flaking plaster, the old archways leading into courtyards, that made me feel I had stepped back into the past.

Every day I visited Moscow's largest and most famous food shop, No. 1, better known as Yeliseyev's, from the name of its pre-revolutionary owner (it still exists and is still called by its old name). It was lit by great crystal chandeliers, and its furnishings suggested an age when women wore bustles and men sported high hats and watch-chains. I went to GUM, a large department store opposite the Kremlin on Red Square (it, too, is still very much in use). Its design of three-storey-high, glass-roofed arcades with fountains was reminiscent of London's Crystal Palace of 1851. Moscow's hotels were other relics of a bygone era. Art nouveau swirls decorated the façade of the Metropole; Atlantes—sculpted figures of men—supported the ceiling of the Hotel National's lobby; massive furniture filled its guest rooms, and spittoons adorned the hallways. Elderly, bewhiskered doormen in baggy uniforms trimmed with tarnished gold braid sat at the entrances of the hotels and restaurants.

My feeling of having stepped back in time was strengthened when I discovered that the décor inside many homes was also old-fashioned—if it was not spare and plain. Rooms were decorated with family group photographs, tinted chrome lithographs, sepia photos of Rodin sculptures,

Two generations of Muscovites relax on a park bench during a spell of fine weather. On the left a young couple are absorbed in their own world, oblivious to a group of babushkas, or grandmothers, huddled in gossip.

hearts-and-flowers postcards, tasselled lampshades made from pink, purple, or orange crêpe de Chine.

Much of what I saw was sadly worn or rundown. During the succession of upheavals after 1914—the war, revolutions and civil war—the fabric of the city had been neglected. Masonry was chipped; paint peeling, plaster crumbling. Steps were worn, balustrades broken. After the Civil War, which had ended in 1922, there had been a movement to rebuild Moscow in a truly socialist image ("Streets are our brushes, squares our palettes," wrote the poet Vladimir Mayakovsky, leader of the Left Art Front). The functional modern structures that had been erected during the 1920s, however, were too few in number to counter the image of a down-at-heel city. Every effort was concentrated on constructing factories, as the country rushed to catch up with the age of steel. New factories were mushrooming on the outskirts of the city and old ones were being enlarged.

The factories attracted new human tidal waves, forcing the authorities to ration housing space. Dormitory living and shared accommodation had been common in the mill sections of Moscow prior to the First World War; now communal flats were the general rule, with one family to a room, and several families sharing a bathroom and kitchen. I was lucky to get a room. Single people commonly settled for cots in the factory dormitories, or a curtained-off corner of a room. Shortly after arriving in Moscow I saw scaffolding on top of many existing two-, three- and four-storey buildings: workmen were adding new floors to the old buildings as the quickest—and cheapest—method of easing the housing problem.

Housing was not the only thing in short supply. The empty shop windows told the story of food and clothing shortages. Meat was scarce: the peasants, in their resistance to collective farming, had slaughtered millions of cattle rather than surrender them to the collectives. Flour was hard to come by: much of the grain harvest was being exported to pay for foreign machinery. Black bread, potatoes and cabbage were the staples; sunflower-seed oil was issued in lieu of butter, and jam or sweetmeats—when *they* were available—instead of sugar. A government-issued coupon entitling the holder to buy a sweater, suit, shoes or rubber galoshes was more highly prized than money. Little wonder that women called the net shopping bag they carried everywhere an *avoska*—a "perhaps" bag. Who knew what they might find?

The new factories required power, and electricity was therefore rationed. The penalty for exceeding the electricity quota was a heavy surcharge. If it was levied on the residents of a communal flat, bickering arose over who had left lights burning late at night, thereby causing all the families to incur the fine. It was as hard for a family to get a separate electricity meter as it was to get a private apartment.

Spartan conditions applied to all aspects of life. During my first winter in Moscow, I discovered that the wooden tramcars were unheated. Hoar-

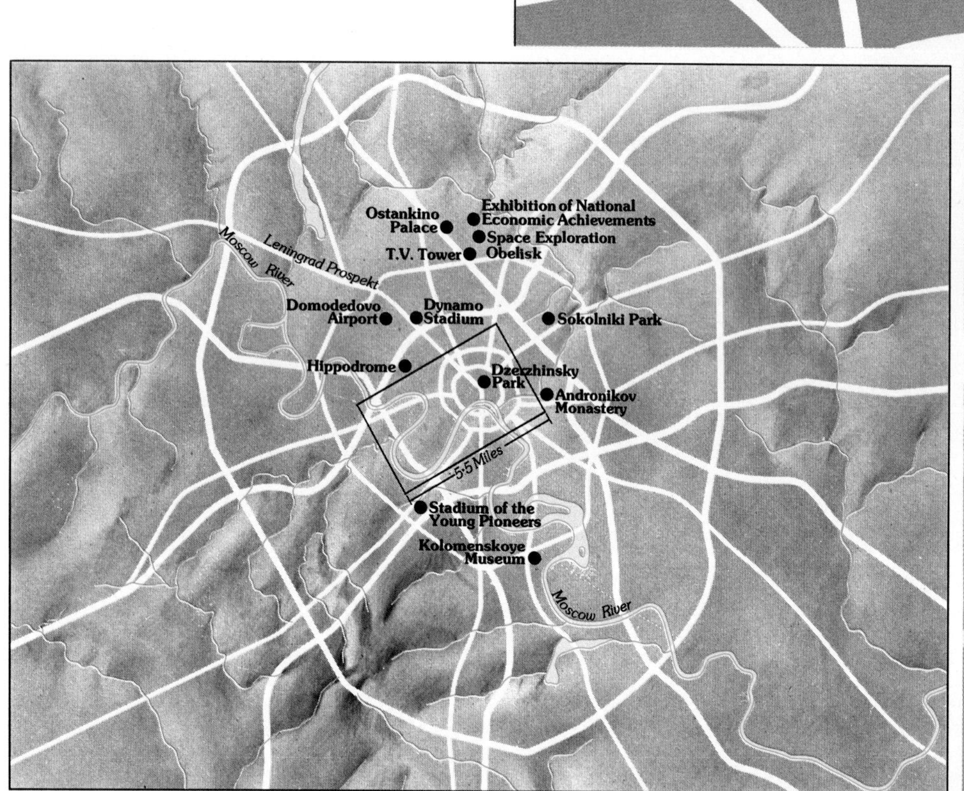

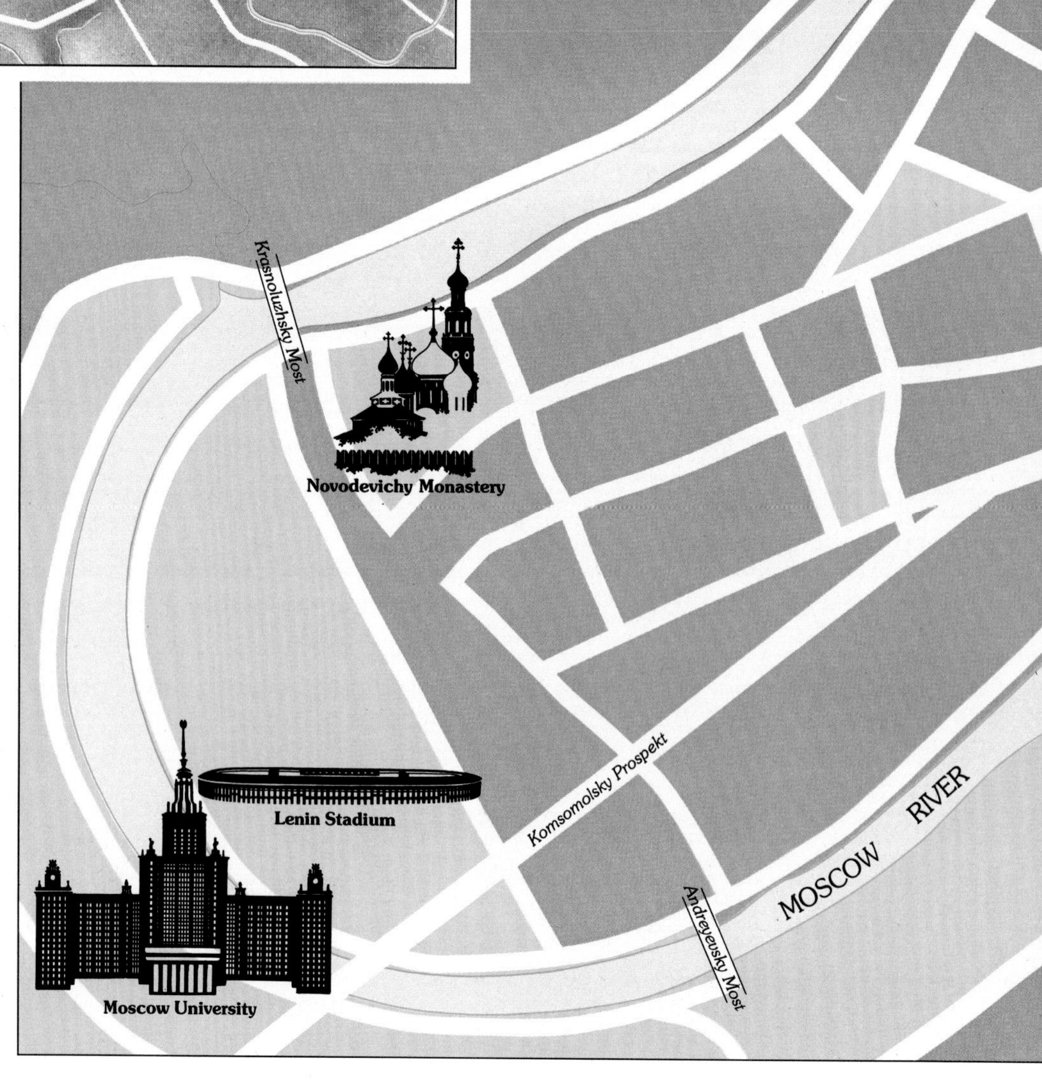

Moscow's Rings of Growth

For centuries Moscow was as much fortress as city, growing behind defensive walls pushed out in widening rings. Most of the old walls have vanished, but they have left their concentric imprint on the city and affect its development today. On the map at right, the areas the walls originally enclosed—gorods—are coloured in different tints. In 1156 a wooden stockade was built to protect the busy little trading community that grew up beside the Moscow River (pink). Over 350 years this was enlarged into the present brick-walled Kremlin (grey). In the early 1500s an earth rampart enclosed the artisans' quarter now called Kitai Gorod (brown). By 1593 the expanding city had a new wall surrounding the Bely Gorod (the blue area on the map), and within seven years yet another wall, which enclosed the Zemlyanoi Gorod (buff area). Today ring roads—the Boulevard Ring and the Garden Ring respectively—follow the boundaries of the Bely and Zemlyanoi Gorods. The last wall erected was a Customs Rampart built in 1745 (encompassing the central area seen in the inset above). Where it stood a railway now girdles the older party of the city.

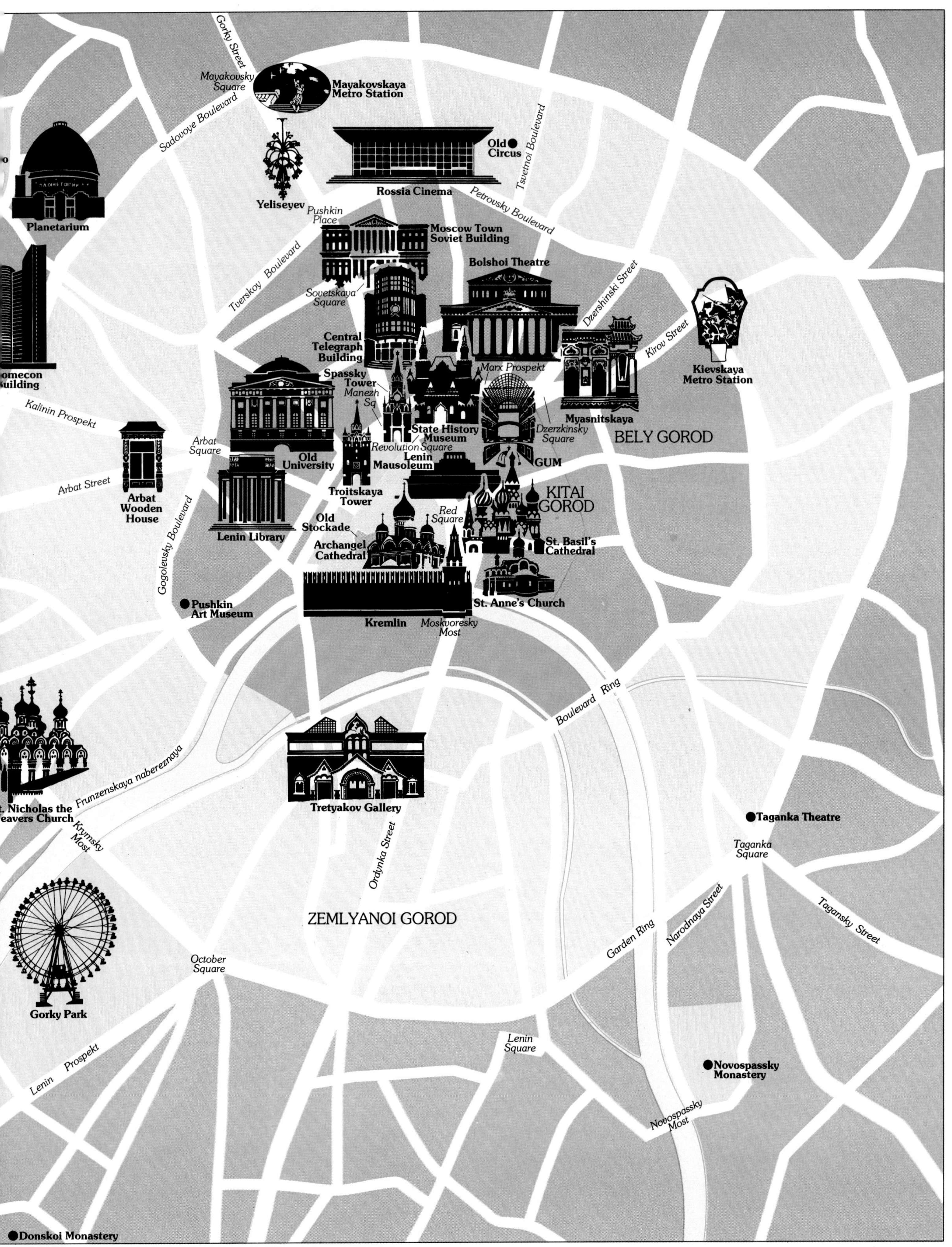

Gorky Street
Mayakovsky Square
Mayakovskaya Metro Station
Sadovoye Boulevard
Old Circus
Tsvetnoi Boulevard
Planetarium
Yeliseyev
Rossia Cinema
Petrovsky Boulevard
Pushkin Place
Moscow Town Soviet Building
Bolshoi Theatre
Tverskoy Boulevard
Sovetskaya Square
Dzershinski Street
Central Telegraph Building
Kirov Street
Kievskaya Metro Station
Marx Prospekt
Spassky Tower
Manezh Sq
Myasnitskaya
Kalinin Prospekt
State History Museum
Dzerzkinsky Square
BELY GOROD
Arbat Square
Old University
Revolution Square
Lenin Mausoleum
GUM
Arbat Street
Arbat Wooden House
Troitskaya Tower
KITAI GOROD
Red Square
Old Stockade
Lenin Library
Gogolevsky Boulevard
Archangel Cathedral
St. Basil's Cathedral
Pushkin Art Museum
St. Anne's Church
Kremlin
Moskvoresky Most
Boulevard Ring
Frunzenskaya naberezhaya
Tretyakov Gallery
Taganka Theatre
Krymsky Most
Ordynka Street
Taganka Square
Taganksy Street
Narodnaya Street
Garden Ring
ZEMLYANOI GOROD
October Square
Gorky Park
Lenin Square
Lenin Prospekt
Novospassky Monastery
Novospassky Most
Donskoi Monastery

frost formed on the inside of the windows, building up into a layer of ice a quarter-inch thick. I learned to scrape a tiny hole in the coating of ice to look out. The conductors—almost all of them women—wore stovepipe-shaped, warm, felt *valenki* boots, padded coats and woollen head-scarves. They managed somehow to collect fares and give change in spite of the clumsy mittens they wore.

Against this background of shortages and hardship, the slogan that I saw plastered over the city, a summons to "overtake and surpass" the West, seemed sheer hyperbole—and so did some of the grandiose construction projects that were then under way. Entire blocks along Gorky Street, leading off Red Square, were being towed back, inch by inch, as much as 45 feet and set down on new foundations—not to create space for housing, I discovered, but to widen the existing road into a ten-lane boulevard for traffic that did not exist.

The most ambitious project was the Metro. The spacious marble stations that were being built for this underground system, many to be bedecked with mosaics, statuary and gold leaf, seemed senseless when I contemplated the shabby housing above ground. Even in the factories there was extravagance of a kind. Expensive machinery had been imported, but the hastily-trained workers often did not know how to operate it, and out of ignorance sometimes wrecked sophisticated equipment.

Foreign tourists, engineers and newspaper correspondents who gathered in the hotel dining rooms ventured all kinds of explanation for such incongruous planning. Some believed that the elaborate Metro and the wide streets were designed to divert the Muscovites' minds from the chronic shortages (circuses instead of bread). Others assumed they were promissory notes, intended to give the public a foretaste of some resplendent, but remote, future. One bizarre notion was that the gleaming Metro stations were designed to teach cleanliness to the influx of peasants. A few shook their heads at the vast streets being laid out and cited Russian historical allegories: the 16th-Century bronze cannon that was so big it could not be fired for fear it would blow up; the Kremlin's ancient 200-ton bell, the world's largest, that cracked and never rang. But some observers were not so sceptical. Several shrewd American engineers pointed out to me that much of the imported machinery, including a Detroit automobile plant sold to Moscow by Henry Ford, was not the most modern or the most expensive, but just the kind "for peasants to learn on".

As time went on, I made some Russian friends. The fact that I was puzzled by such activities and goals puzzled them in turn. They believed that Moscow, as the Caucasian folk poet Rasul Gamzatov put it, was "where the world began". To them the city was open sesame; it promised education and boundless opportunity. But my friends felt more than the attraction that draws ambitious Americans to New York or Britons to

Shoppers crowd one of the three huge galleries of GUM, one of Moscow's largest department stores. Completed in 1893 and partly remodelled in 1953, the three-storey complex still retains its original lofty glass roof.

London. Rather, they felt about Moscow as the French do about Paris—the focus of their country, if not the world. In this highly centralized state, Moscow was "The Centre"; that was the name they unself-consciously called it by. All else was "periphery". In their eyes, Moscow was a favoured city, the pinnacle of urban civilization. It got the best of everything the country had, from books to food. They felt privileged to be there and harboured none of the foreigners' doubts about what lay in store for the city. When I asked them how long it would be before all the vast construction plans were completed, they answered: "Wait."

They accepted implicitly the glowing promise of the future that was dinned into them from large loudspeakers on street corners and from the small, cone-shaped cardboard ones used in apartments and dormitories. The small loudspeakers, wired to central receivers, served as substitutes for radios, and gave forth a stream of bravura symphonies, folk music, marching songs and pep talks. The most common words on the posters were "struggle" and "battle": battle for steel, struggle for machinery; battle for motor cars and a tractor industry, struggle for grain harvests.

Most of my friends were students who, like most Muscovites in the 1930s, were not native-born. One had come from a factory in the Ural Mountains. His Young Communist League unit had sent him to a Moscow *rabfak*, a school that prepared young workers for higher education. He hoped to become an engineer. In those days anyone worth his salt wanted to become an engineer, including women; but his girl-friend, a bob-haired, 19-year-old student of English, told me that she wanted to become either a translator or a literary critic, or, if worse came to worst, a teacher. One of her classmates enjoyed drawing and toyed with the idea of transferring to an art school. She was the daughter of a prominent physician and the only native Muscovite among my friends. In her spare time she coached the family's housemaid in a *lik-bez* course, designed to eliminate illiteracy. In those days, a domestic staff was still employed by some well-to-do professionals. The influx of peasant girls provided a steady supply. The only problem was how to house the maid; usually she had to sleep in a curtained corner off the kitchen or at the end of a corridor. Most maids went on to factory jobs after they had learned to find their way around the city. My friend's maid was still mastering how to read and write.

The older generation must have found the struggle to hasten progress a grim prospect after the privations of the Revolution and Civil War, but to my young acquaintances it was an adventure. They laughed and sang—they sang often in those pre-transistor days—and if they were lucky enough to get balcony tickets at the Conservatory Concert Hall, they sat entranced. Sometimes we went swimming at suburban villages along the Moscow River. My companions did not have bathing suits; the men swam in their underwear, the girls in bras and panties. At beaches that were separate for men and women, they swam naked.

Once I was invited to accompany a student couple when they went to record their marriage at ZAGS, the registry office for births, marriages, deaths and divorces. The office was a gloomy room in the basement of an apartment house. The couple filled in forms, a disinterested woman clerk inscribed their new status on the internal passports that Soviet city-dwellers had to have, and that was that. The bride asserted her right to keep her maiden name. Afterwards there was a party, held in a dormitory, where the guests ate sausage and cucumber, and drank vodka and wine. A tinny phonograph played sentimental arias, then someone produced an accordion and the guests sang. The songs were punctuated by cries of "*Gorko!*" (Bitter!), a signal for the couple to kiss—to sweeten bitterness—while the guests drank toasts to them. I noticed that the girls at the party primly refused the vodka and drank only sweet Crimean wine.

The newly weds did not have their own accommodation, but friends who were on holiday had lent them a room. They expected to be assigned to the same out-of-town construction project when they graduated from their technical institute, or to be given jobs together in Moscow. That was one of the reasons why the couple had registered their marriage: registration gave them the right to work in the same city and eventually to claim a room of their own. Had it not been for these benefits, they might not have bothered to record their marriage. There were many stories of students who married simply to remain in Moscow or to obtain a share in a room, and there were jokes about the suitor whose first question was, "Do you have a room in Moscow?"; or the country boy who married an elderly

The dazzling décor of Gastronom No. 1, a food emporium in Gorky Street, overshadows both the provisions stacked on the shelves and the queuing customers. Still often referred to by the name of its pre-revolutionary proprietor, Yeliseyev, the shop offers a wider variety of foodstuffs—all at fixed prices—than is found anywhere else in Moscow.

widow and, when asked how the marriage was going, replied: "Badly—the apartment doesn't have a view." But the acute housing shortage was the cause of domestic tragedies, too. Although divorce was as easy to arrange as marriage, estranged couples often had to go on living together in the same room because there was no other place for them to stay.

The strain imposed by the first five-year-plan had just begun to ease when I settled down in Moscow. The second five-year-plan promised a relaxation at last. Rationing was lifted from one item after another, and a trickle of consumer goods came from the factories. Peasants in the outlying districts were allowed to tend their own plots when they were not working on the collective farms, and the livestock and produce they raised augmented the government-ordained supplies. By the end of 1934 the last rationing was lifted. Some items that the government food shops still lacked could be found at the peasant markets. Mushrooms, berries, flowers and fruit were the specialities of the markets, where the peasant women chewed sunflower seeds as they hawked their wares.

The most famous of Moscow's old market places, Okhotny Ryad (Hunters' Row), near Red Square, had been torn down at the end of the 1920s and replaced by a new central market on Tsvetnoi Boulevard, almost a mile away. On the spot where stall-owners used to sell game and other provisions, two block-long, 12-storey buildings and a paved square were built. On one side of Okhotny Ryad (today's Marx Prospekt) rose the red-granite and white-limestone façade of a government building, which now houses the State Planning Committee. Across the way was erected the imposing Hotel Moskva, crowned with a roof-garden restaurant.

On the ground floor of this hotel the Tezhe Cosmetics Trust, headed by Madame Molotov, wife of the Soviet Premier, opened a showroom stocked with perfumes and toiletries. Pink Tezhe toilet soap was put on sale in shops, and its synthetic strawberry odour began to replace the smell of laundry soap. The main attraction of the Tezhe shops was perfumes, such as "Red Moscow", which was packaged in a box adorned with a tassel. Every Moscow girl seemed to want perfumes and eau de cologne, but there was less enthusiasm for lipstick. All the available lipstick was of a sickly carrot tint, but that was not the only reason it was shunned. Moscow girls were rather prudish in those days and believed that painted lips were a sign of easy virtue. I remember an occasion at a Moscow theatre when the girl I was with, seeing a heavily made-up foreign woman, whispered to me: "Do you think she's a . . . ?" She did not finish the sentence.

There were other signs of change from the hardship of the first five-year plan. Soviet champagne appeared in Yeliseyev's food store, together with grapefruit and tangerines from Abkhazia in the Caucasus. Muscovites relished the tangerines, but few took to grapefruit. Canned corn and *korn fleks* (a name that later was Russified) also went on sale; but they too won few admirers, in spite of the posters announcing that one can of corn equalled the nutritional value of three eggs. An ostentatious tea shop on Myasnitskaya (Kirov) Street—which the pre-revolutionary owner had decorated in Chinese style, to attract the Chinese regent to be his guest in 1896 during the coronation of Nicholas II—now stocked coffee again, as well as a variety of teas. The Commissar of Trade, Anastas Mikoyan, returned from a trip to the United States in the mid-1930s, and soon after his visit I saw women vendors selling "Eskimoes": chocolate-coated ice-cream bars of the kind known in America as Eskimo Pies or Good Humors. Ice-cream parlours sprang up, and the vendors did a brisk trade on the streets even in winter.

Another innovation that Mr. Mikoyan brought back from America proved less successful at first. His ministry opened a small, experimental cafeteria, near Trubnaya Square, with food kept hot by imported steam tables. The trouble was that by law every portion—even slices of bread—had to be weighed out in grams, and the prices worked out accordingly. Charges had to be calculated down to the kopek, worth much less than a penny or a cent. As a result, each cafeteria customer's bill, running in one-kopek gradations from one kopek (.01 rouble), to ten roubles, was as long as a modern computer print-out and about as complicated. Service was correspondingly slow. Eventually the system was simplified. Instead of an attendant marking up the bill as each dish was handed over, a cashier at the end of the serving line totted up the price of the entire meal with the aid of an abacus.

I found it less complicated to eat at the cafés and dining rooms that were opening up. Muscovites draw a distinction between dining rooms, which provide a simple and inexpensive meal without alcoholic beverages, and restaurants, which are regarded as places for a party or celebration. When rationing was in force, notable restaurants, like the Praga on Arbat Square, had been used as private lunchrooms for top officials. Now they were reopened to the public. The food they served was often good, but rarely as good as that offered in the clubs for writers, actors, officers, journalists, scientists and other professionals.

The trade union and factory clubs had buffets, too; and also concerts, films, lectures and choral and dance groups. At their clubhouses young Muscovites now began to learn modern ballroom dancing—tangos and two-steps, as well as the traditional polkas and waltzes. Girls often danced with girls, as in the Russian villages, and boys with boys. It was common for a girl to invite a boy to dance and an insult if he refused. After the years of proletarian austerity a new song asked: "Why should a young man not wear a bright tie and sigh at the moon?" and the refrain answered that even an earnest Young Communist could do so.

Kultura was a word on everyone's lips at that time. Culture meant a great many things, from wearing a tie to working efficiently ("production culture") and attending the opera. The Moscow opera audiences—many of the men tieless and some in shirtsleeves, the women in print dresses or white blouses and narrow skirts—surged out between acts to stroll or queue at the buffet for open sandwiches and soft drinks. They turned the air blue with the smoke from their long Kazbek and Belomor cigarettes.

The changes in Moscow's diet, mood and appearance came about gradually, but 1935 marked the turning point. The first Metro line opened in the spring of that year; and although it was only seven miles long its efficient service and elegant stations answered my earlier criticisms. That summer the city drew up its first plan for reconstruction and urban development. Most of the population was still concentrated within the Sadovoye (Garden) Ring, which was centred on the Kremlin and only three miles in diameter; but new blocks of flats were spreading out past the industrial districts. Commuter trains, now operating on electric power, carried a heavy flow of *dachniki*, city families who rented holiday accommodation in near-by peasant cottages during the summer. A few trolleybus lines began to compete with the tramcars. The banks of the Moscow River were being lined with granite, and new bridges were built. Gorky Street had been transformed into a wide, modern thoroughfare; cobbled streets and squares everywhere were being asphalted.

Several large glass-and-cement structures—such as the *Pravda* building, housing the main Soviet newspaper; the Stalin (now Likhachev) Automobile Plant's Palace of Culture, and the Consumer Co-operative building on Kirov Street, originally planned by the Swiss–French architect Le Corbusier—were completed. All over town the extra storeys that I had seen being grafted on to older buildings changed the look of many streets from provincial to urban. I found that the architectural finish and proportions of the added storeys turned out to be fairly harmonious. (You can still see these extra storeys in the central part of Moscow, but they are hard to pick out, having been carefully blended with the original structures.)

Muscovites began gradually to lose their peasant image as their dress became more sophisticated. Women still queued at dawn hoping to obtain an attractive pair of shoes before the day's supplies ran out—and they often went home empty-handed; but it was now rare to see anyone wearing ragged shoes made of canvas instead of leather. Head scarves and shawls became fewer; there were more women's hats, mostly cloches or wide-brimmed straws. Ready-to-wear clothing remained of poor fit and quality, but many Muscovites bought lengths of material and had clothing made to measure in the tailoring shops. A fashion salon on Kuznetsky Most displayed styles and patterns.

In spite of the improvements in dress and diet, life remained hard for most Muscovites. The trickle of new housing could not meet the demands of the overcrowded city, and communal flats were still the rule. Illiteracy was largely eradicated, but the schools were so crowded that they had to operate on double or even triple shifts. Health services were free, but some medicines and instruments were in short supply; and the doctors, most of them women, had to make their rounds of house visits on foot. Some worked double shifts to make ends meet.

Whatever hardships the city and its people had to endure, I could not fail to sense the unmistakable air of optimism that the Muscovites projected. Moscow was emerging from the strains imposed by industrialization with the same resilience that had carried it through war and revolution. For me, the climax of those hopeful mid-1930s was the appearance of Grandfather Frost, a Soviet version of Santa Claus. He made his début in Moscow during the New Year school holidays. Unlike the plump Santa of the West, Grandpa Frost was portrayed as a gaunt figure; but he was decked out in a similar red-and-white outfit and long beard, and was just as jolly. He turned up, together with a fairy Snow Maiden, before crowds of schoolchildren at the foot of a towering, sparkling spruce tree in the Hall of Columns, an Empire-style ballroom of the former Nobleman's Club, now the House of the Trade Unions.

Early in 1936 Stalin proclaimed the mood of optimism in the slogan, "Life has become better, comrades; life has become happier." The slogan was all over Moscow. I did not expect to see the outcome of Moscow's great leap forward: I went back to New York that year, hoping to get a job on a newspaper. But America was still in the grip of the Depression, and jobs were scarce. I decided to return to Moscow for another two-year spell, impelled in part by curiosity. How much more had changed?

I was in for a shock. In August, 1936, the first show trial of the great political purges opened. It was staged, ironically, in the same Hall of Columns where Grandfather Frost had beamed upon the children only eight months before. The ominous phrase "enemy of the people" studded the Press stories. My friends were stunned. "Whom can we trust now, if Old Bolsheviks and army generals are traitors?" one asked me in bewilderment. "And if they were not traitors . . . ?" The thought that they might have been framed for political reasons was too frightening for him to spell out. I looked up another friend, but he shunned me: contact with a foreigner might now invite arrest. The roster of "enemies of the people" grew. Night arrests and searches went on. People disappeared and were later denounced as "spies" and "enemies". The purge cast a pall over the city.

I left in 1938. I went back to newspaper and radio work in America, thinking I had had enough of Moscow and Russia, wondering whether Moscow's boom spirit was finished.

Old Square at the Nation's Heart

As daylight fades in Red Square, people still wait before the floodlit Kremlin to visit Lenin's tomb. At right is GUM; at centre, the State History Museum.

Red Square has been the focus of Russian national life since the Middle Ages. Into its broad expanse people crowded to hear the Czar's edicts read aloud—or to watch his enemies put to death. Here, in this century, they came to listen to Lenin speak, and here some of them were killed during the 1917 Revolution. In 1941, on the Revolution's anniversary, Soviet soldiers paraded across the cobblestones past Lenin's tomb, then continued straight out of the city to confront the Nazi invaders; and it was to this spot that they returned in 1945 to celebrate victory. Today Red Square is the vast stage on which ceremonies involving thousands of banner-carrying, flag-waving marchers take place. But even on ordinary days it is packed with people from all over the Soviet Union who have come to pay homage to their country's long history.

A peasant couple, just arrived from the country, walk proudly across the square before St. Basil's Cathedral.

Meeting Place for a Mix of Peoples

Countless numbers of Soviet citizens—from country villages, industrial cities, Central Asian deserts and the icy Arctic—visit Red Square each year. They come to view the colourful domes of St. Basil's Cathedral and to walk beside the Kremlin's ancient brick walls, where niches hold the ashes of Soviet heroes. But above all they come to see the remarkably preserved body of Lenin enshrined in its granite and porphyry mausoleum.

Visitors reflect the U.S.S.R.'s diversity of races and cultures, their faces ranging from European to Asiatic and their dress from traditional to "mod".

A detachment of sprucely-dressed soldiers goose-step past an admiring group of sightseers while completing the hourly changing of the guard at Lenin's tomb.

Snow creates a white halo around the caps of soldiers well protected against the cold by heavy wool overcoats.

The Military on Display

Red Square is the showplace of the Soviet Army, which on special occasions parades its numbers and sophisticated weaponry before the public. The military also maintains a presence around the clock, day in and day out, in the form of two soldiers protecting Lenin's tomb. The precision with which the guard is changed (left) and the motionless figures of the sentries at the entrance to the mausoleum never fail to impress visitors.

While non-privileged visitors patiently wait in line for entry, bridal parties—permitted to jump the queue—leave Lenin's tomb. A Moscow wedding-day custom prescribes that newly weds bring flowers to the tomb. The top of the mausoleum, built in 1930, doubles as a platform for dignitaries during parades.

Photographs of babies blossom above the heads of May Day celebrants.

Pagan Cheer and Political Pomp

On May Day, an old pagan fertility festival that was transformed into a celebration of labour, Red Square is at its liveliest. The annual event used to have a grimly military character, but in recent years it has become more light-hearted. Colourful standards, such as those above, join the flags and pictures of politicians borne through the square by marchers.

A red torrent of flags surges past the History Museum and into the square beyond. Soldiers keep the marchers in line, and ensure they move at a brisk pace.

Fulfilling its historic function as the setting for national ceremonial events, Red Square is flooded with light and people on the night of VE-Day's anniversary. To the left of the onion-shaped domes of St. Basil's is the Spassky Tower, whose clock chimes are broadcast by radio throughout the Soviet Union every day.

2

War and Peace

Moscow has gone through so much in one century—revolutions, civil war, chronic food shortages, purges, war at its very gates—that I marvel it has survived. Of all the vicissitudes the city and its people have experienced, none was a greater nor more hard-won triumph than the Second World War; of their ordeals, none was more exacting than the period of postwar recovery; and of their accomplishments, few evoked more pride than the city's growth since then. I witnessed Moscow's fluctuating fortunes.

I returned to Moscow in 1943 as the field representative of Russian War Relief, an American organization that sent clothing and medical supplies to war-devastated zones. Two years earlier this city of peasant immigrants had managed the impossible: it had turned back the Nazi invaders. In early October, 1941, the German armoured spearhead was within 25 miles of the Kremlin's domes. For several weeks in the frost of an early winter nearly half a million Muscovites, three-quarters of them women, desperately built fortifications and dug tank traps and 400 miles of trenches at the edge of the city. (Thirty years later, my wife and daughter stumbled upon the line of trenches, now overgrown by scrub, while gathering mushrooms near the city limits.) Another 100,000 civilians were sent into the woods to fell timber to fuel the power plants that had been cut off from supplies of coal. Inside the city all the troops that could be mustered, including raw recruits and volunteers, were formed into divisions and sent to the front after only a week's training, with orders to hold off Hitler's 75 divisions until Siberian reinforcements could be brought up. A state of siege was declared on October 20, 1941.

When Napoleon took Moscow in 1812 he was surprised to find that its people had gone and had left him only the hollow shell of the city. Had Hitler taken Moscow, he too would have found it empty of all but guerilla fighters. Some 500 factories loaded their machinery, together with the workers and their families, on to flat cars and box cars, and sent them off to new industrial sites in the Urals and Siberia. A pall of smoke hung over the city as government offices burned their records. During several fearful days and nights civilians jammed the railway stations, where train after train, loaded to the doors with people, set out for unknown destinations beyond the Volga or in Central Asia.

For the duration of the siege the government moved to Kuibyshev (Samara), on the Volga; but although Stalin had panicked at the onset of the invasion, he chose to remain in the beleaguered city. On November 6, 1941, eve of the anniversary of the Revolution (it took place in October

At the grave of the Soviet Unknown Soldier near the Kremlin, a veteran bows his head to the eternal flame. Unveiled in 1967, the memorial enshrines the remains of a young man who died defending Moscow in the Second World War. The trauma of the war, in which some 20 million Russians died, remains strong in the minds of the people. The blocks of granite in the background contain soil from six Russian cities that suffered during the Nazi invasion.

by the old style calendar, but was switched to November when the modern calendar was adopted in 1918), a bomb crater in the lobby of the Bolshoi Theatre forced the celebration to be moved from that traditional site to the Mayakovsky Square underground station of the Metro. There, six carriages on one track served as a cloakroom, and eight on the other track provided a buffet. Stalin addressed the anniversary meeting in the station, with German tanks only 25 miles away. Early next morning Soviet troops converged on Red Square for the anniversary parade, the shortest ever—and they marched straight out of the square to the battlefront.

The city held. When the thermometer dropped to 40° F. below zero, on December 6, Stalin ordered a counter-offensive. Hitler lost 50 of his 75 divisions on the Moscow front during that terrible winter. Not that Moscow's defence had been smoothly planned: there was the usual bungling and bureaucracy. Rather, I think, Moscow simply used everything it had, and it improvised. The spacious Metro stations were used as air-raid shelters. The factories that remained turned out tanks, aircraft and munitions; one of them, Moscow's Compressor Plant, produced the Katyusha rocket launchers that proved so effective against the German panzers. Down the city's wide new avenues rumbled guns, tanks and trucks, headed for the front. Even the plug-in loudspeakers that had served as substitutes for wirelesses during the 1930s aided the city's defence: the network was used for internal broadcasting and provided a ready-made system for alerts and for issuing civil defence instructions.

By the time I arrived, Muscovites were beginning to return to their cold, dark, hungry—but victorious—city. I noticed they had a self-assurance that had been lacking in the 1930s. Even the many who had come from the Russian hinterland and been Muscovites for a decade or less spoke, possessively, of "our Moscow".

I settled into the cold and cheerless Hotel National. I was shivering: whether from actual chill or state of mind or both, I did not know. I tried to warm up by sitting on a radiator, but it was tepid, as all Moscow radiators were during the war. I put on sweaters and fleece-lined gloves, but even that did not help. Finally I went out into the gathering dusk to walk.

The streets, so crowded when I had last seen them, were silent and deserted. The buildings and pavements were painted in complicated camouflage patterns; some buildings were boarded up. I noticed that windows were taped to prevent shattering during bombings, although there had been no air-raids for more than a year. The shop windows were vacant except for war posters.

As I wandered about the city, I saw an occasional elderly watchman or civil defence guard—bundled up in a sheepskin coat; with rifle slung over shoulder—standing in a doorway. I noticed black smudges on the walls of buildings, just above the windows—smoke marks from wood-

The Pervasive Emblems

Moscow is everywhere emblazoned with the symbols of Communism and the Soviet Union: the crossed hammer and sickle, which signifies the unity of workers and peasants, and the five-pointed star. The motifs appear on buildings, on gates and fences, and on people (at left in the top row is the badge of an army officer's hat; in centre of top row, that of a naval officer). There seems to be no limit to the materials of which they are made—including mosaic tiles above the entrance to Moscow University (middle row centre), concrete, on a Second World War memorial (bottom row right), and even stained glass and neon lights in the large modern sculpture seen at top right

ЕСТВЕННАЯ ВОЙНА

burning stoves. Muscovites straggling back from the evacuation had installed the stoves in their unheated rooms. They called them by the name given to the pot-bellied models of Civil War days—*burzhuika*, bourgeois lady—but these new versions were simply square, tinplate boxes no bigger than my typewriter. For fuel the Muscovites had to resort to slivers of wood, the legs of old chairs or any other combustible material they could get—even books. The stovepipes led out through the small hinged pane that Russians open to air their rooms in winter, while the rest of the window is kept sealed to keep in warmth.

Darkness descended. The city was blacked out. I was about to turn back when I realized that I was near a street where a friend had lived before the war. I found the building and started up the staircase in darkness. Behind me came the sound of footsteps and a guard's challenge: "Who goes there?" For a second I was dazzled by the beam of a torch, then it was switched off. I explained that I was looking for a friend.

"No one lives here now," the guard said and turned on his torch for an instant. I caught a glimpse of official seals on each door on the landing. A cold wind blew in the hallway. "There was a bombing here," the guard said, "Come back in the daytime."

I came back the next day and indeed found the building unoccupied, all the flats locked. No one in the surrounding buildings knew what had happened to my friend or his family. Months later I was walking down a street near my hotel when I saw my friend's wife. Her husband was at the front, she told me, and she and her mother-in-law had been evacuated to a village on the far side of the Volga. There they had spent a hungry year. At first she had been a schoolmistress, but after giving birth to a boy she had earned a living by teaching peasant women how to knit. When the two women had returned to Moscow, they found that the building in which they used to live was empty and uninhabitable. The bomb damage had been minor, but water pipes had burst in the untended and unheated building. They moved into a vacant basement room near by.

I visited them there. The basement window panes were broken at ground level. Melted snow had seeped on to the floor and frozen into a thin coating of ice, except around the stove, where it formed a puddle. We sat huddled in our overcoats and talked. When night fell they lit a *koptilka*, or "smoky", a crude wick lamp without a mantle. They had been told that heat and electricity would be restored soon.

My friend's wife and mother were thin and pale. Astonishingly, the baby was plump. In the village they had bartered part of their rations and city clothing for milk from the peasants; and in Moscow they got milk rations for the baby, mostly in the form of Lend-Lease powdered milk. This wartime child seemed to be flourishing, and in spite of the cold and hunger the adults were undaunted. All they could think of was victory: When would it come? How soon? The enemy held most of their country west of Moscow, but they had no doubt that victory would be theirs. "Had not Moscow held?" the older woman said. "Well, then?"

They were cheerful. They laughed and joked about the possible ingredients of the black bread that was their staple diet and about the *burzhuika* and the "smoky", until I, who had been depressed by all around me, became cheerful too. We ended the evening by drinking a toast to victory, in unsweetened tea. Welcome back to Moscow.

The first of many artillery salutes boomed out over the city in August, 1943; it celebrated the recapture of Orel, 200 miles south-east, and Belgorod, nearly 300 miles south-east of the capital. Throughout 1944 the salutes and firework displays marking Russian victories helped build up morale. The streets became busier as more Muscovites returned from the evacuation. Theatres reopened; the Bolshoi Opera and Ballet played to full houses. I cannot recall any war plays; it was too soon, the playwrights were at the front as correspondents—and who wanted to see a play about the war that they were living every day? Music was a different matter; in 1944 the Conservatory Concert Hall offered a succession of cantatas, oratorios and symphonies on patriotic themes.

Wartime Moscow was predominantly a city of women; the men were all away fighting. Everyone worked ten and 11 hours a day, often in cold, gruelling conditions and often hungry. For most people the daily ration was approximately two pounds of black bread, and even this was given only to manual workers or persons with a higher education. Lend-Lease egg powder was a substitute for meat. Dates, when they were available, were used as a substitute for sugar. Many Muscovites raised green onions in window boxes, snipping off a bit of stem daily to chew for vitamins.

There was no longer the casual attitude towards common-law marriage that had prevailed before the war. Only registered marriages were officially recognized under a 1936 law that made divorce and abortion difficult to obtain. Now, when Muscovites sang *Meadowland*, a popular song about the boys going off to war, they omitted the verse about the girls' tears and sadness. Always there was the haunting dread of a postcard announcing the death in action of a loved one.

The constant awareness of death brought many into the churches. Before the Revolution Moscow had more than 400 churches, but after the seizure of power by the Bolsheviks their bells had been stilled. The atheist campaigns of the 1920s and early 1930s had succeeded in shutting most of the houses of worship and, according to one estimate, the rebuilding of the city had done away with half of them. Later, even some atheist writers deplored the loss of the churches as architectural landmarks. One such writer listed 14 outstanding churches of the 17th Century that had been destroyed (some were demolished to make room for car parks), including the famous Kazan Cathedral dating to 1630, near Red Square. The

On the perimeter of Moscow, women dig trenches in preparation for the city's defence in October, 1941.

Women at War

As Nazi troops advanced on Moscow in the autumn of 1941, the entire population was mobilized. Men were rushed to the front and children were evacuated to the country; but many of Moscow's women remained to help defend their city. On its outskirts they dug trenches and tank traps, often under danger of enemy aircraft fire; after air raids they dealt with bomb damage and repaired vital railways. Ably filling places left vacant by fighting men, they also kept munitions factories running and operated the city's transportation network. Their hard work and determination, evident in these pictures, played an important part in keeping the Nazi army at bay and saving Moscow.

Files of cheerful and determined female auxiliary troops—many of them in casual dress—lead their rifle-carrying sisters-in-arms on a training march.

Church of Christ the Saviour, one of the largest in the land, erected in celebration of Napoleon's defeat in 1812, was so sturdily built that the wrecker's ball was of no avail against it, and it had to be dynamited. Stalin dreamed of building a skyscraper Palace of the Soviets on the site, but the scheme was abandoned. Instead, an outdoor heated swimming pool 426 feet in diameter occupies the site today.

Stalin needed the support of organized religion to help unify the country during the war. The church gave it unstintingly, as it has done repeatedly when invaders threatened Russia. A score of Moscow churches reopened, and by the end of the war the total in operation had risen to about 50—a number that has remained fairly constant ever since. The public packed them all. At Christmas and Easter, crowds filled the streets around the Yelokhovsky Cathedral, waiting patiently to get into the church.

As an American, I was constantly being asked when the Western Allies were going to launch the Second Front. The Muscovites' impatience grew close to bitterness under the burden of their wartime sacrifices, but it melted when the Allied forces landed in Normandy in June, 1944. That winter, the victory salutes mounted in frequency and on VE-Day all the pent-up feelings—pride, joy, hope, friendship—welled up in Moscow. At dawn that morning youngsters began streaming towards Red Square, followed by older folk. They filled Red Square and soon adjacent Manezh Square, where the United States Embassy occupied what is now the Intourist office building. For one brief, wild moment in history, all bars were down between Muscovites and foreigners. The Moscow crowd cheered, danced, sang, surrounded every uniformed man and tossed him into the air. Then they started on us—"us" being every Allied citizen they encountered—hugged and kissed us, and roared themselves hoarse with glee beneath the twinned Soviet and American flags. For one marvellous day between World War and Cold War we were all caught up in the illusion of peace—and no doubt frightened the hardline Communist ideologists with our demonstration of mutual warmth.

But when the lights went on again after the war—a few weeks after the announcement that the Americans had exploded a new type of bomb with the destructive power of 20,000 tons of T.N.T.—the barriers went up again. And the Muscovites turned back to a painful reality. Moscow was bleak. The shops were empty; only sparse traffic drifted down the broad streets. The city faced an appalling task of reconstruction, for it had to rebuild its hard-won age of steel at the same time as the country raced to catch up with the atomic age. There were postwar purges ahead. The dream of a better future was postponed.

With the war over and my job done, I went home to America once more at the end of 1945. But Moscow had entered my blood. When the wartime alliance between the United States and the Soviet Union gave way to the open rivalry of the Cold War, it was obvious that we had to learn everything

An architect's model of the Palace of the Soviets is all that remains of Stalin's proud scheme to erect the tallest skyscraper in the world. Planned in the 1930s as a government office building, the structure was to have risen 1,161 feet, and been surmounted by a 200-foot chromium-plated statue of Lenin. In 1941 the building's steel skeleton was torn down to be used for defence materials, depriving Moscow of the grandest example of what is today referred to as "Stalin-Gothic" style.

we could about Russia. But as Stalin embarked on a new round of purges, Soviet censorship became so severe that foreign correspondents in Moscow were sometimes prevented even from quoting *Pravda*. In 1949 I established *The Current Digest of the Soviet Press*, an American weekly journal of translations of Soviet publications. It outlasted Moscow's censorship of outgoing dispatches (which relaxed after Stalin's death and stopped in 1961). *The Current Digest* is now published from the Ohio State University, but for its first 20 years Columbia University was its host. From there I followed Moscow's changing fortunes during the final years of the Stalin era and the rise of Krushchev.

In 1956 Khrushchev startled Muscovites with his "secret" speech exposing Stalin's purges. The speech was never printed inside the Soviet Union, but Party members were instructed to spread its contents by word of mouth. They read it aloud or paraphrased it at meetings in almost every Moscow factory and office. "Rehabilitated" survivors of the purges returned to the capital from prison camps. The Moscow magazine *Novy Mir* printed Ilya Ehrenburg's *The Thaw*, a novel that presaged a flood of exposés and gave a name to the period. Moscow was emerging from the Stalin freeze.

At the end of the 1950s I went back for a visit to see the changes for myself. Traces of the war were still visible—a preponderance of women, men wearing their old army coats, war veterans on crutches—but the city was unmistakably on the move again. Russian friends proudly showed me the first two buildings that had been erected in Moscow after the war. Symbolically, the exteriors were faced with some of the granite that

Hitler, when he expected to capture Moscow, had sent with his troops to build a Nazi victory monument. Gorky Street was now a thoroughfare lined with shops and neon signs. A ring of seven "Stalin-Gothic" towers, reminiscent of the Woolworth Building in New York, punctuated the Moscow skyline. Above them rose the 994-foot-tall central tower of Moscow University perched on the Sparrow (now Lenin) Hills. Below the university, across the Moscow River, a new stadium had been built. Called Luzhniki Stadium, it could accommodate 100,000 spectators. Beyond these massive buildings wide avenues ran past the outer limits of the pre-war city and were being extended across the surrounding plain.

From 4,500,000 in 1939, the population had risen to 6,000,000. To satisfy the demand for housing it was no longer enough to graft extra storeys on to buildings in the centre of town. Entire new neighbourhoods were being erected on the south-western fringe of the city as part of a second long-range plan of urban development. Khrushchev had decreed that there were to be no more of the ornate, slowly built Stalin-Gothic structures. Instead, cranes swung prefabricated concrete panels into place to form rows of monotonous, five-storey blocks of flats: box-like buildings that were five storeys high because that was the tallest size practicable without installing lifts.

Tar-like seams scarred the buildings where the panels were joined. The new developments had insufficient shops and services, and the streets in these new sections were seas of mud; but my friends now talked of exchanging one room in town for a two-room flat in the south-west.

New metal trams replaced the rickety wooden ones, and petrol and diesel buses sped down the city streets, emitting black fumes from low-grade fuel. Occasionally, I saw a crippled war veteran driving a two-seater invalid car with hand controls. Taxis mingled with streams of olive-coloured army trucks converted to peacetime use. As traffic increased, underpasses had to be constructed so that pedestrians could cross the 12-lane streets in safety, and the police at last became strict with jaywalkers.

In the centre of town a few red or green neon signs enlivened otherwise drably-lit streets. "Glory to the Communist Party," some proclaimed. "Buy a state lottery ticket," others urged. "Fly by aeroplane," Aeroflot inanely advertised. There were other signs that announced stores and restaurants. In place of the plug-in loudspeakers, transistor radios were all the rage, and roofs sprouted television aerials. The apartments were overheated, as if the Muscovites were compensating for the chilly war years.

The character of the Muscovites had changed, too. They retained their love of the soil. (What Muscovite does not engage in Sunday gardening or mushroom picking, or keep a summer cottage or at least seek out the city's huge, unspoiled parklands?) Nonetheless, they were now urban, if not urbane. Moscow was increasingly a second-generation city: the sons and daughters of the former peasant immigrants were now technicians and professionals. As the capital of this extraordinarily centralized state, Moscow had always attracted a high proportion of the bureaucrats and managers who ran the country; but now the "scientific intelligentsia" formed an important element of its population. My friends' sons and daughters flocked to the glamorous new profession of physicist as eagerly as their parents had flocked into engineering. Scientific and industrial research institutes lined Lenin Prospekt, one of several great boulevards built in the 1950s.

My friends were saving to buy the small Moskvich and Pobeda automobiles, and complained of the three- or four-year waiting list for them. Ramshackle home-made garages constructed of scrap boards and sheet metal began to disfigure the fields around the new suburbs and even invaded courtyards in town. Some of my friends were building their own summer cottages, the *dachas* of Russian tradition, or investing in co-operatives that erected colonies of these country homes. The *dacha* zone, up to 50 miles from Moscow, was too far for year-round commuting. Moreover, most of the summer cottages were little larger than the one- and two-room flats in town, and few were habitable in winter. All the same, they were a welcome supplement to the trade union-sponsored resorts, providing breaks from the city for hundreds of thousands of Muscovites.

Some of my acquaintances boasted glossy, much-sought-after Czech furniture, which they proudly exhibited to me. Other friends told comic stories about the gaucherie of the newly "arrived". The most common concerned the *Generalsha*, the general's buxom wife. She bought a grand piano, for instance, and when the tuner said it lacked resonance, she responded, "Never mind, my husband will buy some."

At the same time, an aesthetic leavening was apparent. Superb concerts of Baroque chamber music drew new audiences, and poetry readings could pack large stadiums. It was the halcyon time for a whole generation of young Moscow poets and balladeers, among them Yevtushenko, Voznesenky, Okudzhava and Akhmadulina. Pushkin Square overflowed on the annual Poetry Days when they recited their verses. On Mayakovsky Square the rebellious young gathered in the evenings and on Sundays to recite anti-Stalinist poems and to argue with the armbanded Young Communist police aides who tried to disperse them.

The young were displaying a new freedom in styles and behaviour. The 1957 International Youth Festival had brought hordes of young foreigners to Moscow for the first time, and the youth of Moscow had picked up some of their ways. With the increasing importance of the Soviet Union in world affairs, Moscow's diplomatic colony grew and, together with the increasing flow of tourists, brought a renewed foreign presence to the city. Early cultural exchanges with the West—an American production of Gershwin's *Porgy and Bess* was one of the first—whetted the Muscovites' interest in

A Home of Their Own

Although the Soviet government heavily subsidizes housing, hundreds of thousands of Muscovites still live in some sort of communal quarters. For somewhat more affluent or privileged Moscow families there is an alternative to the cramped conditions and the long waits for bigger flats: co-operative privately owned housing—such as the 16-storey block in south-west Moscow where these photographs were taken.

A dining table is the centrepiece of a Moscow cook's flat.

These journalists surround themselves with music and books.

Although co-operatives are, in fact, encouraged by the government, they still only comprise about 7 per cent of the city's housing. The purchaser makes a 40 per cent down payment, and pays off the remaining amount in monthly instalments over 15 years. In addition, he bears the monthly costs of maintenance of the building.

Small families of up to three people share a standard unit—comprising bedroom, living room, kitchen and bathroom—whose prefabricated uniformity, as seen here from approximately the same vantage point in each living room, soon takes on the personalities of the proud homeowners.

A ministerial office worker proudly stands in her living-room.

Two engineers and their daughter enjoy their new furniture.

foreign culture; and Moscow clothing manufacturers began to copy East European fashions, which were themselves copies of Western modes. In defiance of their elders' conservatism, young women took to wearing slacks; and *stilyagi*, youths given to extravagant foreign modes, frequented another import—the new "*Kokteil holl*" on Gorky Street. This street earned the title "*Brodvei*", a designation later applied to the new Kalinin Prospekt. Short-lived cafés, which offered jazz, sentimental or satirical ballads, and poetry readings, sprang up, as well as two daring theatres: the Sovremennik (Contemporary), which dealt with bold new themes, and the Taganka, which in the early 1960s revived the declamatory style and the bare, impressionistic stage of the 1920s.

The workman's cap had been the common headgear for men in the Moscow of the 1930s. A felt hat, sign of the intellectual, could bring the jeering epithet *shlyapa!* (hat!), meaning an impractical fop. But in the Khrushchev era most men took to wearing broad-brimmed felt hats. Sometimes, however, like Khrushchev himself, instead of creasing the top they punched the crown in front, creating the ludicrous effect of a bashed-in derby. Many men wore buttoned-up shirts without ties. Their baggy trousers and the mannish blue serge jackets and skirts of the women made a seedy impression. But the crowds moved briskly. Moscow was catching up.

I returned to daily journalism, and an American newspaper assigned me to Moscow as its correspondent in 1972, eight years after Brezhnev came to power. After a succession of erratic Khrushchev reforms, the Brezhnev period offered stability. "Normalcy", American correspondents called it. The new administration tried to still Moscow's intellectual ferment and concentrated on material problems. I realized how sweepingly they had approached that of urban development when I saw the city again. It had long ago burst the bonds of its four-mile diameter of the 1930s and then its eight-mile diameter of the 1950s; now it formed an oval that was 17 to 23 miles across. The population had risen to 7,500,000, a jump of a million and a half since my previous visit, and the authorities were trying to deflect some of the headlong increase towards a ring of satellite towns beyond the *dacha* zone.

Half-a-million Muscovites a year were moving into new housing. The city closed the last basement flat. Some of my acquaintances now lived in co-operatives, which were superior in design and construction to the municipal housing. On the fringes of town, at the edge of the 65-mile Belt Highway that now encircled the city, the architecture at last showed touches of colour, trim and diversity. Muscovites who once welcomed the five-storey developments of the 1950s now scorned them as *Khrushchoby*, a pun on Khrushchev's name and the word *trushchoby*—slums. A number of my friends moved to the outskirts, where cranes were putting up prefabricated buildings 16 to 22 storeys high. Each of these blocks took only

Aelita, a painter and fashion designer, adjusts a sleeve on one of her creations. Her gowns, which are made from fabrics hand-painted by her to suit the personality of the wearer, are popular with singers, actresses and concert musicians in Moscow.

three or four months to build; fleets of cranes were at work on dozens of them at a time. After the buildings were erected however, it was often another year before they could be tenanted. Some were so hastily constructed that they required repairs before they could be occupied.

Families of four or five now enjoyed the luxury of three-room private flats, although several hundred thousand Muscovites still remained in communal flats, awaiting their turn to move. The space per person had increased from a 1914 average of six square yards to about nine (exclusive of bathroom, kitchen and hallways); but the goal of a separate room for each adult, a separate flat for each family, and 13 square yards of space per person lay in the future.

Modern conveniences were common. Central heating plants, operating chiefly on natural gas piped from fields more than a thousand miles away, supplied most of the city with steam heat and hot water. Around the corner from the old State Bank, in the city centre, country women still clustered on Friday evenings to sell bundles of leafy twigs to bathers entering a *banya*, one of the public bath houses; and I saw this scene repeated at a score of other bath houses. But the public *banya* had largely yielded to the tub or shower at home, and the habit persisted only among those who regarded a visit to the bath house as a social occasion where one could enjoy an evening of steaming the pores, beating the body with leafy twigs to stimulate the circulation, and afterwards quaffing beer while cooling off.

My Moscow friends took gas cookers for granted, and they boasted vacuum cleaners and refrigerators. Several had washing machines, outmoded barrel-shaped models topped with wringers, and looked forward to buying the semi-automatic models that came on sale in the early 1970s. Other Muscovites made do with self-service launderettes, which were always crowded, and laundries, which often filled the day's quota of shirts within an hour of opening, causing many in line to be turned away. Dry-cleaning establishments, which bore the name *Amerikanka* because of their American equipment, did a thriving business.

The Muscovites were respectably attired, and sometimes a striking outfit caught my eye on the street or at the theatre. Several talented Moscow designers catered to the new sartorial awareness. One, the artist Aelita, created original, hand-painted fabrics, and designed gowns for concert singers and wives of the élite. Most Muscovites, however, were in pursuit not of originality but Western styles—and they were always a few years behind trends. The men wore very narrow-brimmed felt hats, almost Tyrolean in style; in the 1970s they caught up with the fad of jeans and flared slacks. Girls ignored the newspaper articles that criticized hippy modes, and started to wear minis about 1973 and maxis in 1975, in bright new fabrics that were slowly displacing monotonous flowered prints. An American friend remarked admiringly on the display of legs in minis; I commented on the new fabrics of the maxis. He laughed. "You've become a Muscovite," he said. Platform shoes and knee-length boots for women, which came into fashion in the West at the end of the 1960s, gained popularity in Moscow during the mid-1970s. As I wrote this I suddenly realized: I had not seen a man in a belted peasant smock for a long time.

Weddings were a far cry from the one I had witnessed at ZAGS in the 1930s. A special store stocked bridal gowns, together with house furnishings for newly weds. To gain admission to this shop you had to present your marriage licence. The busiest counters in the jewellers were those selling wedding rings. Wedding Palaces offered formal civil ceremonies, with champagne and beribboned cars for the wedding party.

Bathers now wore bikinis, and a few sported beach ensembles. As the city spread, swimmers moved up river to new beaches. A canal built in the 1930s had connected the Moscow River with the upper Volga, creating several new river ports in Moscow and assuring it a water supply. Dams erected along the waterway formed a chain of lakes and reservoirs, each of them five to ten miles long. New resorts and *dacha* colonies arose along their banks. As the city encroached on the woodland, large tracts of forest were preserved as parks. Now the first lawn mowers came into use along city boulevards, but in the parks the grass grew refreshingly tall. Along the Garden Ring the municipal authorities had removed the tree-lined centre lanes in order to widen the boulevard to gargantuan size, but the Muscovites admitted that the mania for huge traffic arteries at the expense of greenery had been a mistake, and along the newer boulevards the authorities began planting trees, lawns and flower-beds.

The city was brightened up at night as well. Fluorescent lights illuminated the main streets, department stores and cafés blossomed with neon signs, and neon strips outlined tall buildings. One lone three-storey-high advertising sign, with about half a million electric bulbs, was erected in Mayakovsky Square in 1974. It resembled the billboard signs of Piccadilly Circus and Times Square. The lights formed animated cartoon figures to advertise taxi services, air travel, newspaper subscriptions, and occasionally spelled out political slogans, including Brezhnev's "Make Moscow a Model Communist City".

Indefatigable women street cleaners continued to sweep the pavements with besoms and to hack at the ice in winter, but modern street cleaning machinery now kept the thoroughfares clear of snow. "Stalin claws"—trucks with crab-like pincers—scooped up the snow piles; in summer, fleets of watering trucks swept the boulevards regularly. Municipal transport was fast and still cheap, the highest fare being five kopeks. The Metro had been extended into a web of a hundred immaculate stations, each one architecturally distinctive. The buses, although crowded, were heated and of the "pay-as-you-enter" type. I still choked occasionally at the black fumes emitted by trucks and buses, but I saw several pilot models operating on natural gas cruising the streets; and one day I spotted an experimental electric minibus on Marx Prospekt. A fleet of about 15,000 taxis supplemented the public transport system.

By the mid-1970s Moscow had some 100,000 trucks and buses, 50,000 company or government passenger cars, and 200,000 privately owned cars—not many compared with the millions in New York, Paris or London, but enough to create the first Soviet traffic jams. Officials who travelled by company and government automobiles were being told to learn how to drive so that the number of chauffeurs might be reduced. Higher officials had large limousines, and the police kept central lanes clear for them, directing the other traffic with baton gestures as elaborate as the twirling of drum majorettes. The only limousines as large as those of ministers and Party leaders were those of foreign diplomats and a few Western bankers. Bankers? Yes, Wall Street banks had opened offices on Marx Prospekt, the city was building an international trade centre, and foreign businessmen were as common in Moscow as foreign engineers had been in the 1930s. Even so, Moscow had—and has—a small population of foreigners compared with that of Western cities.

Many doctors now made their rounds in cars belonging to the clinics. The Moscow ambulance service was so much faster than its equivalent in American cities that U.S. medical research teams chose Moscow as the best place to study the treatment of sudden heart attacks. One evening, on a street in the university district, my wife and I encountered a woman who was bleeding heavily. She had fallen through a window. While I called an ambulance from a public telephone, a crowd gathered. The bystanders muttered indignantly about the slow ambulance service, although the ambulance arrived in 11 minutes, with oxygen and blood transfusion equipment. The bystanders were still complaining when the patient was taken off to "*Sklif*", the Sklifosovsky emergency hospital.

About that public telephone. When I first came to Moscow, most of the city's telephones were of the old, wooden-handled type. I cannot recall seeing any public phone booths, although they certainly existed. At the start of the 1960s dial instruments replaced the old-fashioned type and telephone booths were common. The drawback was that many Muscovites were hoarding the two-kopek pieces they needed for public phones; sometimes it was harder to get the correct coin for a call than to find a phone. In 1974 the meters were modified to accept one-kopek coins as well, and the problem was solved: one of those trifles that matter in Moscow.

Characteristically, Moscow solved this problem only to be faced with another. Now there were plenty of public phones and they took a variety of coins, but only 50,000 copies of the four-volume telephone directory—the first in a decade, listing more than a million entries—were published, and they were sold at a price of more than 20 roubles for each set. A copy was not to be found in public places. Few Muscovites possessed one, few

As a violinist plays and friends look on, a young couple in formal dress register their marriage with an official of one of Moscow's three Wedding Palaces.

even knew the directory existed, and most continued to jot down numbers without checking their accuracy. As a result, Moscow telephones seemed to ring more often with misdirected calls than with the right numbers.

Buildings long neglected got coats of fresh paint in the mid-1970s. Many of the old-fashioned buildings remained, but they now seemed to me like historical or period pieces amid modern settings. Many institutions that occupied historic structures gained modern premises or new branches. The Art Theatre obtained a large second building half a mile from the old; and the outworn Tretyakov Gallery of 1906 prepared to move to a streamlined, air-conditioned new home farther from the centre of town. The turn-of-the-century Old Circus building, remodelled in the 1930s, was augmented by a big circular, glass-and-aluminium building, the New Circus building out in the university district. GUM, the State Department Store on Red Square, erected in 1890, and TSUM, the Central Department Store, were enlarged, and joined by a dozen other department stores scattered about the city. The old Grand Hotel was surrounded and absorbed by the granite-and-marble Moskva Hotel. The elegant Hotel National, where I had stayed during the war, was refurbished and preserved, but at its back rose a 20-storey hotel—the Intourist. The 3,200-room Rossia, the world's largest hotel—the ten-acre "Big Box", as Muscovites called it—was built just outside the Kremlin at one end of Red Square, to rival the outmoded 1903 Metropole near the other end. Inside the venerable Kremlin walls a 6,000-seat, glass-walled Palace of Congresses housed productions too large to be staged even in the 2,155-seat Bolshoi Opera and Ballet Theatre. Some critics dismissed the Palace as "pop art hung in a Renaissance gallery", but most Muscovites took pride in its spacious modernity.

In short, to return to Moscow was to face the surprise of a modern metropolis. When I spoke of my reaction and described the Muscovites' pride in their city, Western visitors looked askance. Surprise—in the age of atomic energy and supersonic aeroplanes? What was so surprising about this metropolis, what was so modern about it? They pointed out that the shops, with their limited variety of goods and long queues, were depressing. Much of the new housing was shabby, with floor tiles broken loose in the lobbies and other signs of disrepair. The city had efficient rubbish collection, but public toilets were in a shocking state. Those frequent and inexpensive buses were so crowded at rush-hours that you risked your coat buttons when squeezing in or out. People queued for hours in the vain hope of gaining admission to cafés and restaurants. As one correspondent quipped, this was a city where restaurants locked their doors when they opened for business.

Looking back on this description of Moscow in the 1970s, I note that it is studded with qualifications. Washing machines, but outmoded; laundries, but inadequate; telephones, but no public directories. By omitting the reservations and qualifications I could paint a glowing picture of the city—and propagandists do. By concentrating only on all the "buts" and "howevers" I could indict the whole scene.

Securing a spare part or garage space for a car was a lengthy task. Spares were so difficult to obtain that Moscow drivers, when parking, habitually removed windshield wipers, to guard against their theft. The planners rushed the city's buildings to completion before they awoke to the need for underground garages. Some drivers poured vodka or gin into their car radiators because anti-freeze was often unavailable. The Muscovite might pride himself on his ambulance service and clinics, but he would wait in line for hours to fill a prescription for eyeglasses, only to be told that the necessary lenses were unobtainable. At a privileged no-waiting service garage for diplomats I waited for a month and a half for replacement of a simple plastic tail-light housing for my Soviet car. It was that peculiarly Russian thing: "a deficit item".

There were always shortages of one kind or another. Coping with them was a way of life, part of the price Moscow paid for its rush to catch up with the West. The city that could build the superb Metro and the world's tallest television tower could not produce baby bottle nipples and seat belts for cars. The inconveniences came of trying to accomplish more than was feasible and to do it faster than conditions permitted. The city was so busy expanding and the nation so involved in forcing economic growth that there never seemed enough left over for the amenities of living.

I needed only to read the Moscow newspapers to learn all the shortcomings. Muscovites resented the foreigners' criticism of their city's failings, but were themselves harsh critics of Moscow's faults. And yet their city was miraculous to them—because it was new and fast growing, but most of all because of what it had cost them through the years. It had many things to boast of, yet what impresses the Muscovite sometimes seems a curious matter for pride. Of what other city was it noteworthy that stores stocked bridal gowns and that families at last were getting three-room apartments? For myself, I have only to cast my mind back to the peasant immigrants in the railway station in 1933 to understand.

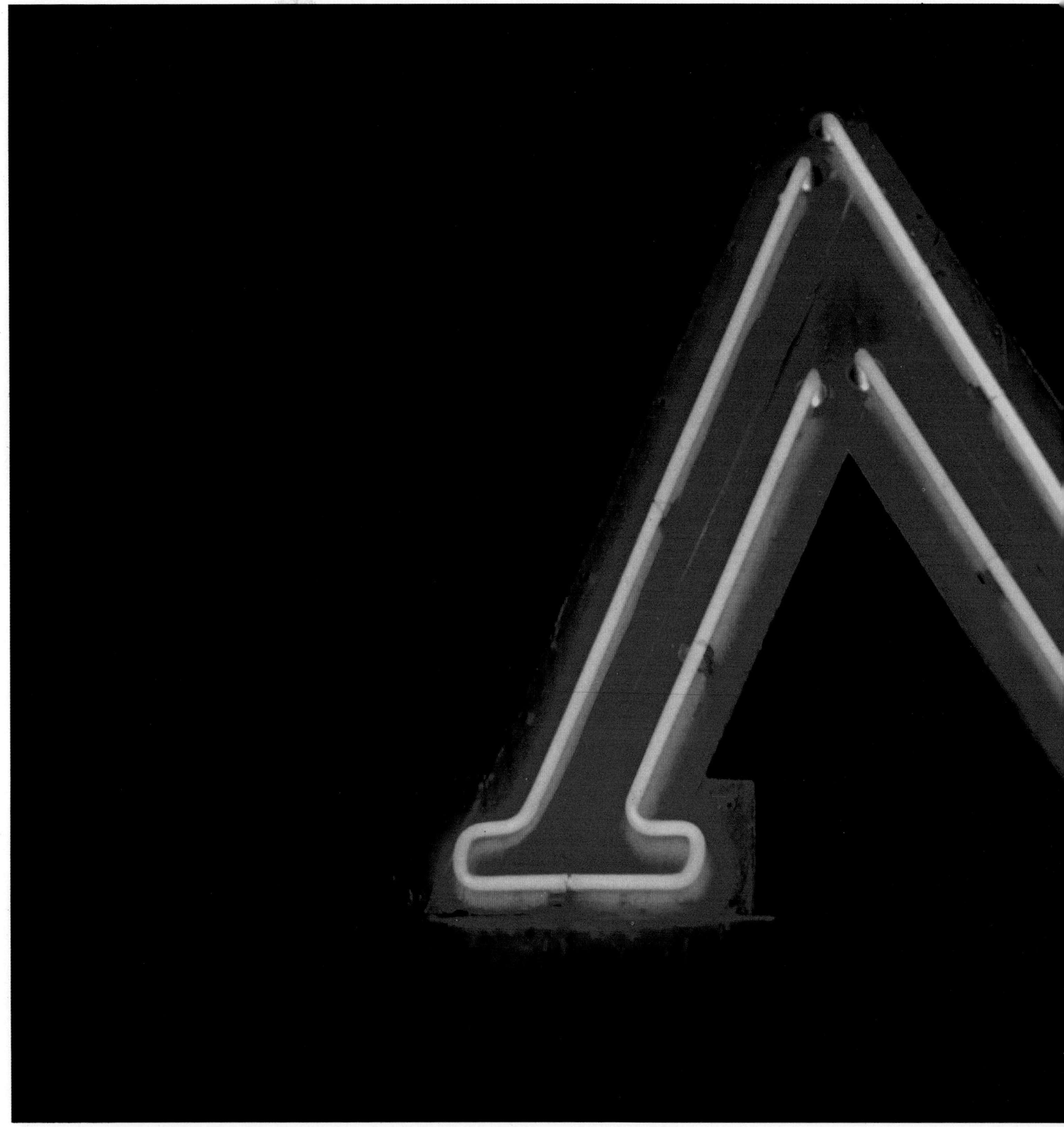

Underground Palaces

PHOTOGRAPHS BY PETE TURNER

A neon "M", motif of the Moscow Metro, glows in the night. Signs such as this, about two feet high, stand prominently above the entrances to each station.

Moscow's underground, the Metro, is justly famed as one of the city's most magnificent achievements. Conceived by Stalin in the early 1930s as a prestige venture, the subterranean network was built by a workforce of 60,000 men and women labourers and 5,000 engineers (partly under the supervision of Nikita Khrushchev, who later went on to become leader of the Soviet Union). The first stations, inaugurated in May, 1935, and several that were opened soon after, dazzled Muscovites with their cavernous spaces, brilliant lighting and opulent decoration. The extravagant use of marble, mosaics and statuary was in marked contrast to the austerity prevalent elsewhere in Moscow. Stations built later were designed on a more modest scale, but their precursors set a standard of opulence never again approached anywhere else in the world.

Passengers walk along an ornate passageway in the Kievskaya Station.

Chandeliers for the Proletariat

As the Moscow commuter descends underground by staircase or escalator, he leaves behind the dour face of Moscow and enters a sumptuous world. In the Kievskaya Station (above), passages glow with soft lighting. Ironically, the chandeliers, with their gilded decorations and frosted-glass shades, bring to mind the ostentation of the pre-revolutionary age.

Even with a train standing at the platform, Kievskaya Station, with its chandeliers and sculptured archways, has the appearance of an elegant drawing room.

In a main corridor of the Revolution Square Station, opposing pairs of bronze figures—idealized versions of Soviet citizens—crouch beneath the arcades.

Pantheon of the Revolution

Each of the Metro stations has its own unique character and style. While some are palatial in décor, others are spare and monumental. In the Revolution Square Station (above)—dedicated to those who fought in the 1917 Revolution—the architectural terseness serves to complement the heroic Soviet theme: a series of bronze sculptures of muscular men and women, all representing builders of the Soviet state in attitudes of alert readiness.

Statues in the Revolution Square Station include a frontier guard and his dog, an architect at work, a sturdy sportswoman and a rugged pioneer.

The designs of the stained-glass panels of Novoslobodskaya Station derive partly from the traditional motifs found in old Russian embroidery and tapestry.

A Secular Church

The grandeur of the Moscow Metro is due largely to the theatrical use of marbles of many colours brought from quarries all over the Soviet Union. A staggering 70,000 square metres of marble were used in the first 14 stations—more than in all the courts built by the Romanovs over 300 years. In combination with brightly lit, stained-glass panels—as in the Novoslobodskaya Station (above), completed in 1952—the effect is churchlike.

A stained-glass roundel set into one of Novoslobodskaya Station's colourful panels offers a neatly dressed, thoughtful Russian at work in his tidy office.

The illuminated ceiling niches on Mayakovskaya Station platform visually echo the rows of arches.

Ceilings that Glorify Valour

Sophisticated lighting in some of the Metro stations makes the traveller forget he is often hundreds of feet underground. The gleaming and spacious Mayakovskaya Station (above), built in 1938, was one of the first to employ innovative lighting techniques. Its fluorescent fixtures soften the lines of the massive ceiling, and the long rows of slim, stainless steel pillars, picking up and reflecting the light, add to the impression of an airy vista.

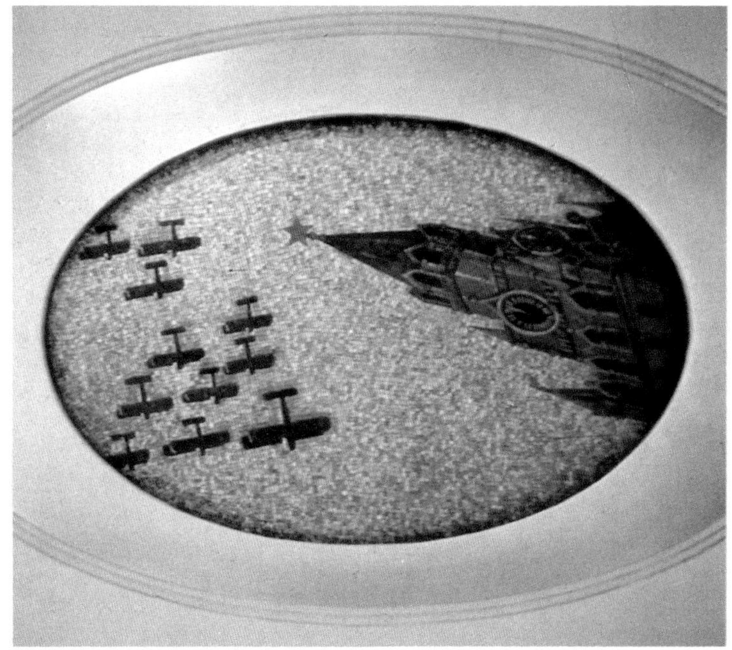

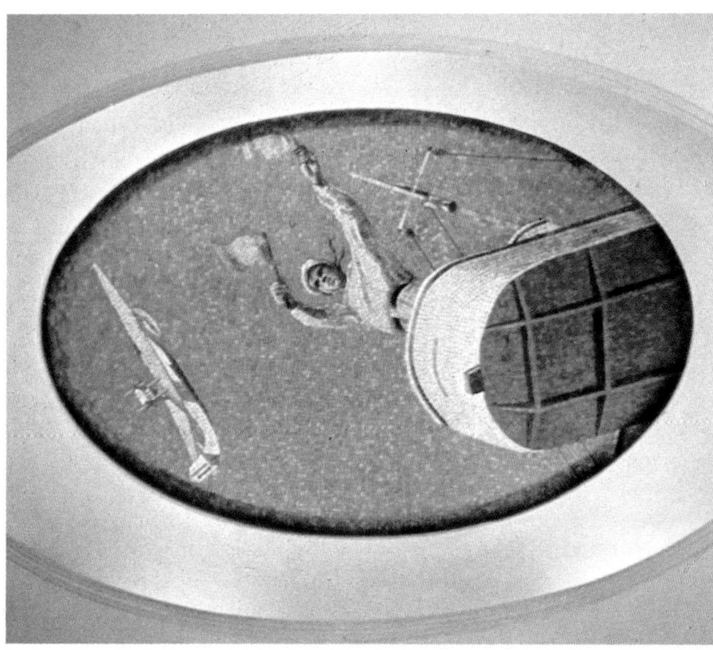

DICK ROWAN

Within the floodlit domes of the Mayakovskaya Station are oval mosaics that represent "A Day in the Soviet Sky", symbolic of Soviet conquest of the air.

This mosaic of medieval warriors is from the station ceiling seen at right.

A Proud Glitter

One of the most baroque of Moscow's stations is the Komsomolskaya (right). It took its name from the near-by square, which was dedicated to the Komsomol, or Young Communist League, whose members provided labour in the early years of the Metro's construction. Its mosaics and paintings commemorate people and events from Russia's military past.

Komsomolskaya Station boasts all the elements that make the Metro world-renowned: decorated ceiling, chandeliers, mosaics, pillars and gleaming floor.

3

Discovering the Past

So quickly has the new Moscow sprung up and spread out from the city's former boundaries that I—even as some Muscovites do—tend to get lost in the new sections of town. Although supplied with directions by a helpful policeman, I still have difficulties reaching my destination: block after block may lack street names and be described instead as "Subdivision No. 3", or "4" or "5". Each subdivision in turn may have several sections and each section several buildings. Often, having arrived at the right building, I discover that it consists of several units, one behind the other (sometimes separated), and each unit may have three or four entrances.

Why not carry a street map? You cannot buy a detailed map of Moscow nor, for that matter, of any city in the U.S.S.R.—only sketchy, schematic layouts of the main streets. To fill the gap, Moscow is dotted with information booths where, for a few kopeks, you can obtain directions or track down persons who have moved. To obtain an individual's address, however, you have to submit not only his full name, including the patronymic—the middle name derived from the father's: Ivan Ivanovich (son of Ivan) Ivanov, for example—and his former address, but also the place and year of his birth. The last requirement seemed ridiculous to me until I learned that Moscow has nearly 100,000 Ivanovs, of whom more than a thousand are named Ivan Ivanovich.

Even in older parts of Moscow it is quite easy to lose your way. This is because many old street names have been changed—so many that Moscow newspapers have protested. I once calculated that about 1,500 streets had been renamed since the Revolution, and my count was surely incomplete. Some names were changed to eliminate reminders of the old régime and the Orthodox church, some to honour revolutionary heroes, and some for no clear reason at all. Why change Hunters' Alley to Carpenters' Alley? And yet this was done.

Some changes, I must admit, eliminate confusion. At the time of the Revolution, Moscow had 17 streets named Resurrection, 14 Czar Streets, nine Alexandrovskayas, nine Pokrovskys, eight Trinity Streets, seven Alexeyevskayas, seven Church Streets, seven Bathhouse Lanes, six Nameless Lanes, five All-Saints', four Dirty Streets, four Crooked Lanes and three German Streets. While reducing confusion, the authorities introduced a few duplications of their own. Barely had the city eliminated the name Gagarin Lane, so called after an early 19th-Century householder, when another Gagarin—the cosmonaut Yuri—inaugurated Soviet space flight and a near-by square became Gagarin Square.

Scaffolding indicates where careful restoration and maintenance work are in progress on the brilliantly painted Terem Palace, glimpsed between two other buildings in the Kremlin. Built in 1635-6 under the first Romanov Czar and then later altered and added to, the palace is one of the oldest parts of the Kremlin to have survived the periodic fires and invasions of Moscow's chequered history.

Among the old street names that survive and call the past to mind are Blacksmith's Bridge, Cooks' Lane, Tablecloth Street, Weavers' Street, Fish-Stew Lane, Crooked Alley, Coachmen's Street, medieval Armour Street, Cannon Street and Tar Lane. Fortunately they are not Moscow's only reminders of the pre-revolutionary city. In spite of neglect and the zeal of early Soviet city planners, quite a few charming buildings of Czarist days also survive. And something quite pleasing has begun to happen: they are being restored, including many of the churches the Soviets either shut down or put to uses other than worship.

This new respect for the past came about none too soon. There was concern among some Muscovites that the city fathers were bartering their city's individuality for a mess of concrete. In the 1960s conservationists began to question the headlong craze for construction, and set up a clamour to conserve and restore what remained of the pre-revolutionary city's colourful and historic buildings. The chorus of indignation was led by a writer, Vladimir Soloukhin, who protested that in place of "the most original city on earth", the Muscovites had erected an undistinguished town, "a city like any other, even a good city, but nothing more".

In the early 1930s there actually had been talk of razing old Moscow and building afresh. Instead, the government ordered that the existing city be modernized. In justice to the planners, it should be said that although they ruthlessly demolished churches, bell towers and in general any old buildings that stood in their way, they also took pains to preserve numerous landmarks, including the great convents, mansions and monasteries that are now museums. During the Stalin era, when rash demolition proposals sometimes came from on high, it took courage to oppose them, at the risk of life or liberty, but a few Muscovites did dare. The Young Communist League's newspaper, *Komsomolskaya Pravda*, disclosed in 1965 that during the Stalin era there had been plans to demolish St. Basil's Cathedral, Moscow's most famous landmark, to accommodate auto traffic on Red Square. Pyotr Baranovsky, a specialist in restoring antiquities, threatened to commit suicide if the scheme were carried out. Baranovsky was arrested for his protest but was released when plans for the destruction of St. Basil's were abandoned.

Of buildings that survived, neglect and heedlessness had already taken a heavy toll. Under the pressure of the dual shortages of living and working space, some churches and grand old structures were at the time converted to housing, storage or office use, or grew dilapidated through sheer lack of labour and materials for maintenance. Where old buildings were torn down, new, large, often undistinguished structures went up.

Only briefly, during the 1920s, while Soviet architects were carried away by the still recent revolutionary break with the past, had they turned to functional and constructivist forms. But their efforts were premature and doomed. Moscow possessed neither the modern materials nor the con-

Although it is so cold that he needs a warm hat covering his ears, a craftsman works with ungloved hand—for accuracy of touch—as he restores the decorative plasterwork on a historic building. The care of Moscow's architectural heritage, once neglected in favour of ambitious development schemes, has been given high priority since the mid-1960s.

struction technology to foster experimentation, and the results were discouraging. For example, Soviet officials retained the internationally renowned Swiss-French architect Le Corbusier, but his plan for a bold skyscraper had to be modified to meet the limitations of Moscow's building industry and wound up as a modern but not daring eight-storey, block-long office building. In recent years, moreover, one of its innovative features was eliminated, when its open ground floor was closed in.

The neo-classical reaction set in during the 1930s and carried over into the 1940s, culminating in Stalin-Gothic architecture. Some Westerners ascribed the style to the dictator's predilection for the pretentious; a few considered it ideologically determined. I cannot help but remember, however, that at one time American cities too built "Gothic skyscrapers". The Soviet poet Vladimir Mayakovsky visited the United States in the 1920s, and commented that American builders "bespattered the skyscrapers with musty Gothic and Byzantine embellishments that look utterly out of place . . . like tying pink bows on an excavator or putting celluloid dolls on a locomotive". The description fits Moscow's Stalin-Gothic.

Stalin-Gothic eventually gave way to a more modern design approach, but very little sparkle or originality surfaced. Much of the new Moscow is either pompous, as in the gilded statuary of the fountains at the Exhibition of National Economic Achievements, or nondescript. After the brief experiments of the 1920s the city's architecture began to hit its stride only in the 1960s and 1970s with such large ensembles as Kalinin Prospekt's 20-storey office buildings, all set at angles to the street.

The old Moscow that the conservationists set out to save could indeed claim to be an original city, even if it were not, as the writer Soloukhin said, "the most original city on earth". For it was entirely the product of its turbulent history. In the 12th Century, there was no Moscow, only a stockade—located on the site of the Kremlin today—whose inhabitants benefited from the rich commerce that passed along the river between northern Europe and Byzantium in the south. For protection from marauders, the stockade was turned into a fortress—the original meaning of the word "kremlin"—and the early settlement that became Moscow eventually grew around it. The fortress was not strong enough to withstand the 13th-Century armies of nomad warriors—the Mongols—who swept out of Mongolia on swift ponies to conquer Russia, China, Persia and India. One of these armies, the Golden Horde led by Batu Khan, descendant of Genghis Khan, overran almost all of Russia and burned Moscow in 1237. The town was slowly rebuilt, but survived in thrall to the Horde. The nomad Mongols did not install themselves as rulers; they lived apart, only visiting the town to collect annual tributes. To this day, a Moscow thoroughfare running southwards from the Kremlin bears the name Ordynka, which means highway to the camp of the Golden Horde.

The golden domes of the Cathedrals of the Assumption (near right) and the Annunciation (to left) rise glittering from the heart of the Kremlin. Completed in 1479, the Cathedral of the Assumption, a marriage of Byzantine and Italian Renaissance architectural styles, was for four centuries the scene of coronations. The smaller but no less imposing Cathedral of the Annunciation was built about 10 years later as a private chapel for the Imperial family.

The Mongol occupation lasted for 250 years and effectively cut Russia off from Europe just as the Renaissance began. During its isolation, Russia created a separate culture, centred upon the Orthodox Christianity of Byzantium; the religion became a unifying force against the Horde. Moscow's Kremlin and other citadels like it in Russia developed into strongholds of the church, sheltering chapels and monasteries behind their battlements. Outside their walls, fortified monasteries were built in turn not merely as religious centres, but as defensive outposts. Their bells sometimes summoned the people to pay tribute to the Horde, sometimes to arm against its punitive raids.

The Russians looked to distant Byzantium as the fountainhead of the faith that sustained them under the Mongol yoke, and from Byzantium stemmed the icons and church architecture that are so typical of old Russia. The icons, with their large, wide eyes, golden halos and elongated figures, became objects of veneration. Russian churches also borrowed the round Byzantine domes, adapting them to the snowy conditions of the north by converting them into onion-shaped cupolas. Nearly 700 years later, when Soloukhin sought to describe the unique nature of old Moscow, he singled out "cupola architecture" as its hallmark. "One may like or dislike cupola architecture, as one may like or dislike the minarets of ancient Samarkand," he wrote, "but there is no other Samarkand on earth, and there was no second Moscow."

Byzantium fell to the Turks in 1453. In 1472 Ivan III, Grand Duke of Muscovy, cemented the tie with the Byzantine heritage by marrying Zoe (Sophia) Palaeologus, niece of the last Byzantine emperor, and proclaiming Moscow to be the "Third Rome", heir to the fallen Byzantium. He adopted for its emblem the double-headed Byzantine eagle that looked both east and west. Under Ivan's successors, Muscovy led the Russian principalities in ousting the Mongols, gathered together the Russian lands and spread the Russian domain eastwards as the Mongols retreated. The Grand Dukes of Moscow became the Czars—the Caesars—of all Russia.

During Ivan III's reign, the Kremlin was expanded. Between 1485 and 1495 its brick walls took their present outline: a triangle about half a mile long enclosing some 70 acres on the brow of a hill overlooking the Moscow River. Ivan brought architects from Italy, instructed them to follow Russian models, and set them to building the magnificent cathedrals and palace buildings around the Kremlin's Cathedral Square. Century by century, his successors added chapels, churches, a belfry, towers, cloisters, an arsenal, palaces, theatres, imperial apartments and government buildings—all within the Kremlin's walls. In front of the Kremlin at one end of Red Square (called "Red" since long before the Revolution, because in Old Russian "red", "main" and "beautiful" were the same word; and this main square *is* beautiful) Ivan IV erected St. Basil's Cathedral to commemorate the final defeat of the Mongols in 1552. St. Basil's is a fantastic collection of

Eight Centuries of Trauma and Growth

1147 First mention of Moscow in Russian chronicles

1156 A wooden citadel or "kremlin" is built at Moscow

1220 First invasion of Russia by Mongol hordes

1237 Mongols burn Moscow

1280 Daniel, son of Alexander, Prince of Novgorod, becomes first Grand Prince of Moscow

1296 Kremlin fortified with earthen wall and oak rampart

1325 Accession of Ivan I as Prince of Moscow. Adopts subservient attitude to khans (rulers) of Mongols

1326 Moscow becomes residence of Metropolitan (archbishop) of Russia

1328 Ivan I receives title of Grand Prince of Vladimir from the khans, and gains control of other principalities

1367 Kremlin fortified with stone walls

1453 Constantinople (Byzantium) falls to the Turks, leaving Moscow as the chief centre of Christianity in eastern Europe.

1462 Accession of Ivan III, the Great, first prince of Moscow to be called Ruler of All the Russias

1480 Ivan III refuses to continue paying tribute, successfully repudiating vassalage to the khans

1485-95 New walls expand Kremlin to its present 70-acre size

1547 Ivan IV, the Terrible, crowned Czar and Grand Prince of All the Russias. First prince of Muscovy to use the title Czar (Caesar)

1553 First printing house opens in Moscow

1554-60 St. Basil's Cathedral built by Ivan IV, in thanksgiving for defeat of Mongols in 1552

1598 Accession of Boris Godunov as Czar

1604-13 "Time of troubles"—civil wars in which boyars (nobles), Poles and Swedes compete for throne

1605 The pretender "False Dmitry I" seizes Moscow

1612 Poles occupying Moscow at the invitation of the boyars are dislodged by nationalist uprising

1613 Mikhail, first of the Romanovs, elected Czar

1682	Accession of Peter I, the Great
1712	Peter transfers Russian capital to his newly built St. Petersburg, leading to decline of Moscow
1745	Completion of customs ring round Moscow. Goods moving in and out of the city taxed
1755	Moscow university, first in Russia, founded
1762	Accession of Catherine II, the Great
1776	Foundation of dance company later to become Bolshoi Ballet
1812	Napoleon occupies Moscow. The city burns down as he retreats
1813	Reconstruction of Moscow begins
1837	Stock Exchange founded
1861	Serfdom abolished. Influx of manpower boosts Moscow's industrialization
1881	Assassination of Czar Alexander II by revolutionaries
1889-93	Torgovyye Arcades (today's department store GUM) built in Red Square
1897	Moscow Art Theatre founded
1905	Political strike and uprising in Moscow, part of general unrest following "Bloody Sunday" massacre of demonstrators in St. Petersburg
1917	February: Czar Nicholas II forced to abdicate. Provisional Government set up
1917	October: Bolshevik revolution in St. Petersburg unseats Kerensky's Provisional Government. Revolution spreads to Moscow. Bolsheviks seize control
1918	Lenin moves seat of government and Communist Party Central Committee to Moscow, making it once more capital of Russia
1918-22	Civil war between Reds and Whites (Czarist loyalists)
1922	Stalin appointed General Secretary of Communist Party Central Committee
1924	Lenin dies
1930	Lenin mausoleum built in Red Square
1934	Murder of Kirov, Leningrad party secretary. Stalin's reign of terror begins
1935	First Metro line opens
1937	Moscow canal completed, linking the city with the Volga at Ivankovo
1939	Nazi-Soviet non-aggression pact
1941	German forces approach to within 25 miles of Moscow
1945	Victory over Germany celebrated in Red Square. Cold War begins
1949	New Moscow University buildings begun in "Stalin-Gothic" style
1953	Stalin dies
1956	Khrushchev's "secret speech" denouncing Stalinism. "Thaw" begins
1961	Palace of Congresses built in Kremlin
1964	Fall of Khrushchev. Brezhnev becomes General Secretary
1967	Rossia Hotel, biggest in the world, completed.

asymmetrical domes and towers that the Marquis de Custine, who visited Russia in 1839, called a "masterpiece of caprice" and "a box of glazed fruit".

Nowadays, most foreign visitors to the Kremlin—which Stalin's successors opened to the Soviet public in the mid-1950s—get the impression that they are standing in one great museum. In one sense they are right: the Kremlin walls enclose an extraordinary collection of Czarist relics, including the Armoury Museum which is filled with thrones, crowns, armour, tapestries, coaches, gems, gold and silver.

Within the Kremlin, the Czars were wed and crowned, and most of them lie buried here, along with the patriarchs and metropolitans of the Orthodox Church. Here Lenin lived and worked; his body lies enshrined in the red-granite and black-porphyry mausoleum on Red Square. But the Kremlin is not just a pantheon. It is also the seat of government, where Soviet leaders meet in council. I have heard the Kremlin compared to the Acropolis of ancient Athens and the Capitol of Rome; but when I cast about for a contemporary equivalent, comparisons fail. Imagine Canterbury Cathedral, Westminster Abbey, Windsor Castle and the Houses of Parliament combined on one site. It sounds preposterous; yet certainly no country but Russia has one such national focus. The word "Centre" that Russians use as a synonym for Moscow takes on added meaning for me when I stand in the Kremlin, the Centre of the Centre, and review the centuries of Russian history compressed on this one small site.

Outside the Kremlin walls, to the east, grew up the Kitai Gorod, a half-moon-shaped area about half a mile wide that housed artisans and tradesmen. The district took its name from the earthwork that was built around the settlement early in the 16th Century; Kitai came from *kita*, wattle baskets in which earth was packed for fortifications, and *gorod*, which now means city, used to mean an enclosure. The quarter kept its name when masonry replaced the earthwork in 1535. You can still see part of the masonry fortifications behind the Metropole Hotel, at the northern end of the arc formed by the Kitai Gorod. And to the south, near the huge new Hotel Rossia, may be seen several old buildings, including the "English Court" of Ivan IV—Ivan the Terrible. Ivan long nurtured dreams of marrying one of Queen Elizabeth I's ladies-in-waiting or even Queen Elizabeth herself—what a marriage that would have been!—and he provided this dwelling for British envoys and traders who sailed around the North Cape to Archangel, then travelled overland south to Moscow.

By the time Peter the Great ascended the Russian Throne in 1682, Moscow had become the feudal stronghold of the hidebound, quarrelsome nobles, the *boyars*. Peter detested them and their city, a hotbed of intrigues and uprisings against him. Determined to break their power and to bring Russia into the European world, he abandoned Moscow as his capital. In its place he built his "window on the West"—St. Petersburg. His artificially

With light wooden ladders propped against its fragile, old domes, the 17th-Century St. George's Church near Red Square undergoes a painstaking restoration.

created city was in complete contrast to Moscow. It was built on European lines, with long, straight streets and buildings inspired by classical Graeco–Roman models. Moscow remained Russian to the core—which is more than a figure of speech, for the quintessentially Russian Kremlin *is* of course the city's core.

St. Petersburg replaced Moscow as the seat of empire in 1712. A century later much of the old capital burned down during the occupation by Napoleon. The city's fortunes were at a low ebb, but then came the decree that Moscow should be rebuilt. By 1825 a new city had arisen on the ashes of the old.

Aristocratic St. Petersburg looked down on the rebuilt city as "merchant Moscow"—a muddy, sprawling town peopled by ex-peasants and bull-headed grain merchants. The Kitai Gorod became the business district of 19th-Century Moscow. Banks and offices replaced the abbeys and colourful old buildings that once stood there. Today, state trusts and ministries have replaced the banks; and the Soviet Chamber of Commerce has taken over the Stock Exchange. By day the streets are overflowing, by night they are deserted, so that footsteps echo lonesomely, reminding me of night-time streets on the lower tip of Manhattan or in the City of London.

Although most of the old landmarks are gone, I love to roam the Kitai Gorod for the surprises it still holds. Turn the corner of Old Square into tiny Nikitnikov Lane, behind an ultramodern extension to the Communist Party central headquarters, and you come across a church that might have come out of a fairytale—the Church of the Georgian Icon of the Mother of God, built in 1658. Several generations of builders added Moscow Baroque trimmings to the church, so that one historian called it an "encyclopaedia of architectural ornaments".

Moscow's ancient growth can be read like the rings of a tree. From the eastern edge of the Kitai Gorod, settlements spread north and north-west of the Kremlin towards the present Arbat—an ancient word meaning outlying district—and then south across the Moscow River, until at the close of the 16th Century the city comprised a circle extending about a mile beyond the Kremlin. The Muscovites girdled most of this circle with another wall, this one of white-washed brick and white limestone. The limestone provided Moscow with the description of White Stone City, and the circle became the Bely Gorod—the White Enclosure.

The white wall was demolished when later ramparts were built around subsequent outer rings of growth, and at the end of the 18th Century builders were permitted to use its bricks and stones for genteel private houses and government mansions. The wall left its imprint on Moscow's geography, however. "Boulevard", a word related to "bulwark", originally meant the top of a rampart. A ring of boulevards was laid where the white rampart used to run. This is now Moscow's Boulevard Ring.

Much of the section within this ring was rebuilt after the Napoleonic invasion, and this part of the city has a 19th-Century flavour. It savours of the golden age of Russian art, music and literature. Within the ring are Moscow's art galleries; most of the famous theatres, including the Bolshoi, the Maly and the Art Theatre; the Conservatory where Tschaikowsky taught and where Russian birches—his favourite trees—now surround his statue. Pushkin, Gogol, Tolstoy and Turgenev strolled the boulevards, and here stand the monuments to the titans of Russian literature.

There is one thing I cannot forgive the city fathers. Nikolai Gogol, the great 19th-Century author of *The Inspector-General* and *Dead Souls*, spent his last years in a house on the boulevard strip that bears his name. In 1909 the sculptor N. A. Andreyev portrayed him—bent, shrunken, a tormented man—as he was in his final years, when he was desperately writing the second volume of *Dead Souls*, only to burn most of the manuscript. Shortly before the 100th anniversary of Gogol's death, the authorities moved the statue into the courtyard of the house where he died, and where few now see it. On the anniversary itself, in 1952, a new, benign sculpture of the author was placed at the head of Gogol Boulevard. The sculptor, N. V. Tomsky, was himself displeased with the work. The art critics called it banal and superficial, but there it stands.

The next of Moscow's circles stretches a mile or so beyond the Boulevard Ring. An earthen rampart once surrounded it, and hence the area that it bounded was called the Zemlyanoi Gorod, the Earthen Enclosure. Around its rim in the 19th Century houses with large gardens sprang up; today this is the Garden Ring. The term is a misnomer: the earthen rampart is gone, and so are the gardens. All that remains is a circular thoroughfare; even the trees that used to line the centre of the road have been removed to make way for some of the heaviest traffic in the city.

Many of the merchants' mansions in the Garden Ring have been converted into foreign embassies, and most of the nooks and crannies that once delighted me—in the former aristocratic and bohemian parts of the Arbat, for instance—have disappeared. Here and there one comes across a surviving anachronism, such as carvings on an old, one-storey wooden house, or quiet, old-fashioned lanes in the former merchants' quarter across the Moscow River; but for the most part this circle is now filled with substantial apartment houses.

Beyond the Garden Ring lay the old city's outermost wall, the Customs Rampart, which was completed around 1745. The collecting of duties at city gates was discontinued less than a decade later—except for duties on vodka—but the rampart survived into the 19th Century. Eventually part of it was made into a bed for a railway linking the city's nine railway depots. In the circle bounded by the former Customs Rampart lies the district that belongs mostly to the beginning of our own century—and to Russia's revolutionary history. This was a part of town given over to mills,

Austere and functional, the Zuyev Workers' Club, completed in 1929 and exemplifying the so-called "Constructivist" style, represents a brief post-revolutionary experiment in Soviet architecture. Constructivist theories—that the form of a building should reflect its means of construction—were outlawed as "formalism" under Stalin, and only isolated examples of these clean-lined structures survive.

factories and slums—a home to many of the peasants who poured into Moscow after the emancipation of the serfs in 1861. The slums have been razed and replaced by apartment buildings, and some of the industry is now being moved out. This area was the scene of the 1905 uprising which brought about the first cracks in Czarist power. In the Three Hills Textile Mill area, for example, you can find the occasional log house with a plaque commemorating the workers who manned the barricades.

Beyond the Customs Rampart the post-revolutionary city takes over: the miles of new sections have absorbed many former country mansions of nobles and the wealthy, now public buildings. The Soviet planners have preserved the circular pattern of the city's growth and the radial layout of Moscow's main roads: nine major arteries leading to other cities. These roads run from the Kremlin hub like the spokes of a wheel.

There is no need to talk of modern Moscow and its monotonous, strictly utilitarian apartment houses, about which I've already had much to say. What of the fate of historic Moscow? In the 1960s a chorus of voices was raised to save as many of its treasures as possible. The Society for the Preservation of Historic Structures acquired hundreds of thousands of Moscow members. The Ministry of Culture designated some 1,800 Moscow objects and buildings—from an individual milestone to entire convents—as national monuments to be restored and preserved, and then more than doubled the list in 1973. The city allocated a budget of 12 million roubles for the restorations.

To carry out the work the city drew upon the country's army of some 2,000 restoration specialists. Many of them came from Leningrad, where they had already painstakingly rebuilt the palaces gutted by fighting and bombardment during the city's 900-day siege in the Second World War. To prevent discordant construction in the old centre of the town, Moscow resolved to set a limit on the height of buildings there—to the chagrin of several contractors who were starting to build high-rise structures and had to truncate their designs in the early 1970s.

The restorers fanned out from the Kremlin, through the various circles and even into the new sections of town; for as the city grew it flowed past the outlying medieval monasteries: the 13th-Century Danilov; the 14th-Century Andronikov, where Andrei Rublev, the great fresco painter lived and worked; the 15th-Century Simonov; the 16th-Century Novodevichy, the New Convent of the Maiden, where Gogol, Chekhov, and other famous Russians lie buried; and the 17th-Century Donskoi.

Were I to choose my favourite in this historical pageant, I would think first of Novodevichy, where the ghosts of Russia's past haunt the shady lanes. Here Peter I confined his sister, the regent Sophia, after she fostered an uprising against him, hanged 300 of her musketeers in sight of her convent cell, and nailed her lover's hand to the cell door. Here the devout light candles during services in the vaulted interior of Trapeznaya Church; and all visitors, devout and atheist alike, wander among the graves of the notables, from Shostakovich to Prokofiev and from Stalin's wife Nadezhda Alliluyeva, who committed suicide, to Stalin's successor and critic, Khrushchev.

But most likely my final choice would be Kolomenskoye, a 16th-Century village that lies completely surrounded by the modern city. When my wife and I visit the village, we drive out along the Warsaw–Kashira Chaussee, lined by tall apartment houses, and turn off into a side road. Where the road becomes a dirt lane we leave the car and proceed on foot. Suddenly we are in a street of log cottages. We have many times chanced upon a few wooden houses surviving behind great new housing developments; but it is a surprise to come upon a whole small settlement of these houses, each with its country garden and picket fence, in the midst of the city.

At the end of the settlement, the lane leads on through an arched gateway to the Kazan Church, built in 1660. A service is being held; a rich chanting swells out from the interior and we can hear elderly parishioners whispering in the dim vestibule. Farther down the lane, on a grassy slope above the Moscow River, stands a collection of buildings. In feudal times this was the site of the summer residence of the Czars. In place of the great Wooden Palace where Peter the Great spent part of his childhood are log structures brought from far-off places and reassembled here: a hut from Archangel that belonged to Peter the Great, a prison tower from Bratsk, a mead brewery, and a museum containing icons brought from the Solovetsk Monastery in the far north. The faces of the icons, with their hypnotic eyes—so innocent, so knowing—seem to glow in the dark rooms.

In the centre of the field, next to a tower where the Czars kept falcons for the hunt, stands the Church of the Ascension, crowned by a great, pyramidal tower. We gaze across a gully to where the five massive cupolas of the Church of St. John the Baptist gleam in the evening sun. Silhouetted on a hill behind the 16th-Century church, a boy is driving a herd of cows to water at the river's edge. For a moment we forget we are in Moscow.

Then we look out across the river, where the smoke-stacks of automobile plants, chemical plants and machine shops belch clouds of smoke and steam, and beyond to the white apartment houses that rise in tiers against the sky. In the courtyard of the Church of the Ascension stands a cement mixer, and I notice that workmen are stacking bricks, preparing for a renovation job. We walk slowly back to the car and drive home, back through the circles of Moscow, conscious of centuries streaming past, and pursued by a memory of the great, staring eyes of the icons.

Immortalizing the Dead

PHOTOGRAPHS BY DICK AND CLAUDIA ROWAN

Using a mobile platform to reach her husband's memorial, a widow pays her respects in Novodevichy Cemetery. The wall bears the motif of the state, a star.

Even under the Communist régime it is a mark of status to be interred in the cemetery of Moscow's venerable Novodevichy Monastery, burial ground for eminent Muscovites since the 17th Century. In the Arcadian setting outside the monastery walls, politicians, war heroes and servants of the party are honoured with monuments that emphasize the secular nature of Soviet society yet evince the universal desire to be remembered. Some famous figures, including Nikita Khrushchev, are immortalized in statues; others are commemorated with images or sculptures that recall their work or service to the state. Many personalities are cremated, and their remains are placed in recessed walls (above), that one Western writer described as looking like miniature versions of Moscow's postwar housing developments.

A red scarf, emblem of the Communist Party youth arm, decorates the grave of a Second World War heroine.

Images that Outlast Life

Most of Novodevichy's memorials, whether modest or magnificent, have one feature in common: they display a photograph or sculpture of the deceased. Such graphic representation of Moscow's honoured sons and daughters gives the cemetery the air of a hall of fame. This impression is strengthened on Sunday afternoons when sightseers, who come to spot well-known names on the monuments, mingle with relatives of the deceased.

On a granite pedestal, a bronze figure of cosmonaut Pavel Belyaev stands encircled by a graceful stainless steel whorl representing his orbit of the earth.

The grave of a Soviet air ace is identified by a bizarre memento mori—a piece of aeroplane engine salvaged from his fatal crash and mounted on a marble plinth.

In the wintry peace of the cemetery, a three-foot-long model of a Russian tank guards the grave of a major-general who commanded an armoured division.

Reminders of Mourned Warriors

Among the graves of Novodevichy are those of many Russian soldiers, sailors and airmen who lost their lives in combat during the Second World War. In keeping with the traditional role of the military—selfless devotion to the state—the resting places of the warriors are marked not by personal mementoes but by memorials to their service. Often these are explicit—and sometimes bizarre—reminders of the weapons with which they fought.

Flowers left by a loyal friend nestle against the dreamy head of Nadezhda Alliluyeva Stalina, an idealistic, tragic opponent of her husband's brutal policies.

Lingering affection for Khrushchev is seen in a pink nosegay on his grave.

Famous Faces from the Past

Novodevichy is a place where "non-persons"—figures, like Nikita Khrushchev, who have fallen out of official favour—enjoy some recognition. In a graveside eulogy on Khrushchev, his son said: "There are people who love him and people who hate him, but no-one can pass him by without turning to look." The ex-leader's statue (above) ensures that much, at least.

Two stone doves, one fallen in an attitude of death, the other faithfully standing by, grace the double grave of a devoted couple whose photograph is fixed to the tombstone. The birds, protected from the wintry elements by a plexiglass case, are symbols of fidelity.

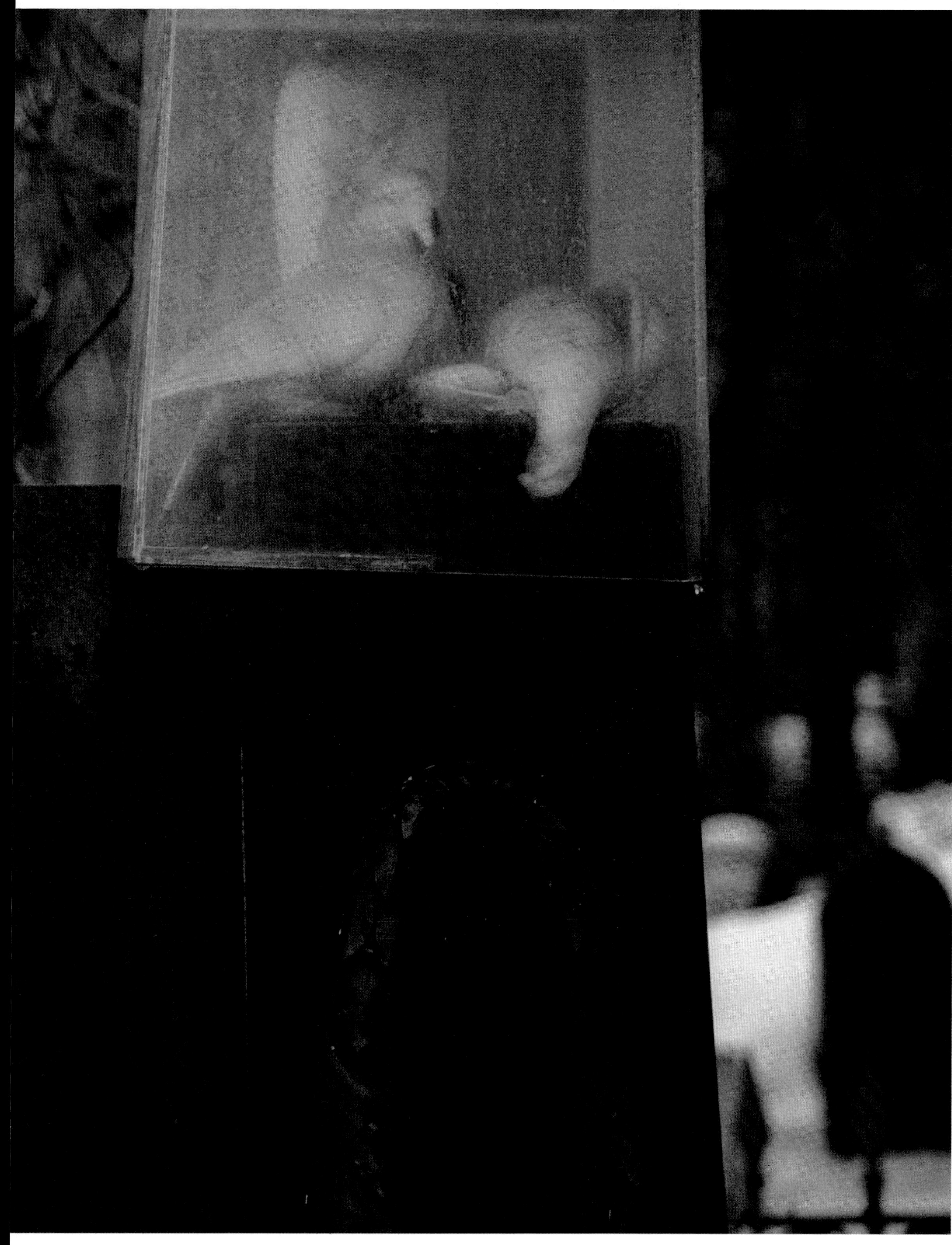

4

Around the Soviet Year

Moscow has a calendar unlike that of any Western city. The passing year is marked not by religious holidays—at least, not officially—but by political celebrations that range from the two- or three-day May Day holiday to dozens of one-day ceremonies in honour of women, children, geologists, cosmonauts—a list that embraces the whole of Soviet society. Nobody could hope to memorize what seems to me to be a calendar of modern, secular Saints' Days. In any case, these events are merely counterpoints to the changing rhythm of Moscow's seasons. The climate of the city fluctuates between such extremes that it has a profound effect on how Muscovites live, what they eat and wear and how they enjoy themselves. I propose to tell you my impressions of Moscow's changing year, as well as describe those events that are special in the Soviet calendar.

When I am far away and try to picture Moscow, I recall a scene from my early days in the city: a snow-clad street observed from my balcony. Soft, blue-white blankets of snow smothered the roofs; mounds were piled along the kerbs like heaps of cotton wool. The hard-packed snow on the pavements, beaten down by innumerable heels, then glazed with frost, looked like hammered pewter. Seen from above, fur-hatted pedestrians swaddled in dark, bulky clothes lumbered along like so many bears. Children on skates darted among them. Little traffic passed down the road; a single car hibernated beneath a heap of snow at the roadside. Occasionally, a squad of soldiers marched down the street, singing. The snow muffled the sound of their boots and muted the song.

It is no surprise that my memory should be a winter one. Soldiers do not march through Moscow nowadays, but ride in lorries; and the hibernating automobiles are kept under tarpaulins in courtyards. The city is no longer blanketed by ice and snow for months on end. Snow ploughs help the army of street cleaners to keep the pavements clear. Nevertheless, winter in Moscow lasts nearly half the year, and to Muscovites it is their season. Most of them regard the first snowfall with the same pleasure that an Englishman takes in a warm, midsummer's day or an American the bright hues of autumn. My own feelings are ambivalent: I love the crisp, frosty days when the whole city sparkles, but hate the long spells of dark chill when the sun stands oppressively low in the sky, casting a feeble light and long shadows.

Winter comes early to Moscow. Snow flurries dust the city with white in early November. But the first few of the 40 snowfalls that Moscow averages annually are only a foretaste of things to come. Not until late

A Russian Orthodox priest leads an Easter procession through the grounds of the old Novodevichy Monastery in Moscow. In spite of Communist Party attempts to discourage religion, the rite—which falls later in the spring than it does in the West—is still an important annual event to many Muscovites.

December do snow and ice begin to dominate the city. That is when children come into their own. Six-year-olds ski in the parks, on skis no more than a yard long; younger children waddle uncertainly along on skates. They are bundled up in so many clothes that they seem wider than they are tall.

Their woollen or fur hats come down to their eyebrows and their earflaps are tied under their chins. The only visible parts of them are the button eyes and button noses peeping out above the thick mufflers knotted round their necks. The men and women caretakers of the apartment buildings sprinkle the courtyards with water when the temperature drops, turning them into ice slides for the youngsters. In freezing weather, park attendants daily flood the paths for the skaters, creating ribbons and loops of ice up to a mile long.

The Russian Orthodox Christmas falls in January, but it is a solemn rather than a festive occasion. New Year is the time when Muscovites celebrate and make merry. The occasion has all the trappings of Christmas, but the gaily decorated fir trees are called New Year trees; Santa Claus is Grandfather Frost and the Snow Maiden takes the place held in some Western countries by the Christmas Fairy. People send New Year, not Christmas, greeting cards, and children receive New Year presents.

Muscovites are allotted about 600,000 New Year trees by the state. In addition to the elaborately decorated giant specimens set up in public parks and clubhouses, and a few hundred thousand that are sold commercially to be set up in private homes, stands of trees are made available at the city's outskirts to Moscow factories and offices, which contract to have allotted numbers cut for their employees. On December weekends I have seen truckloads of workers driving out to the countryside to cut and bring home the quota. Even so, the number of New Year trees usually falls far short of demand, and people heading home with trees slung over their shoulders are liable to be stopped on the street by hopeful strangers asking where they got them and whether any are left. The unfortunates who fail to find the real thing make do with artificial, bauble-covered trees from the city's crowded toy shops.

New Year's Eve is for the adults, who feast and drink late into the night, but New Year's Day is special for youngsters. Early in the morning and all day long the city swarms with parents taking their children to watch performances in theatres, clubs and parks. Many of Moscow's more than 30 theatres put on ten days of children's entertainment during the school holidays at the beginning of January; the chief attractions are the two circuses, the two puppet theatres and the three children's theatres, all of which are sold out a month before New Year's Day. Grandfather Frost acts as master of ceremonies at shows in trade union clubs and park pavilions, outdoors as well as in. My wife and I have stood in parks with chilled fingers and toes watching clowns and fairy-tale dramas. Watching the children is an entertainment in itself. They perch in wide-eyed pleasure on their fathers' shoulders or cluster in front of the outdoor stage. When sweets and other gifts are handed out, the adults are swept aside by the excited crush of children.

After the brief cold spell that heralds the New Year, the skies often become melancholy and the days dreary. What snow does fall is quickly cleared from the main thoroughfares by snowploughs, then collected by lorries and emptied down ramps along the embankments of the Moscow River. Huge rotors agitate the water to send the débris drifting down a channel that is kept open by ice-breakers. The leaden, overcast sky seems to be draped just above the dull buildings. Smoke and steam from factory chimneys only accentuate the pall. The snow that remains on backstreets and in courtyards soon turns a sooty grey. On the busy Garden Ring muddy lorries from country roads and constructions sites churn the snow to a sticky brown paste that coats the windscreens of cars and spatters unwary pedestrians. At such times Moscow has an oppressive air. I walk miserably along the street, head lowered against the chill.

Just a week or two of such gloomy weather and you feel that winter has already lasted long enough. Then, overnight, fresh snow falls and you awaken to a rare sunlit day; the cold becomes bracing, tingling the nostrils, and the frosty air is as clear as glass. On such days my wife and I collect our skis and head for the outskirts of the city.

One of the joys of Moscow is the ease with which one can reach the countryside. We need only to catch a bus or travel by Metro to the end of the line, then walk a short distance until there are no more apartment buildings. A road leads us through the fields and woods that surround Moscow. Occasionally a car or truck swishes past. The road itself has been cleared by a snowplough, but beside it, where we are walking, the snow crunches underfoot, and gets deeper and softer as we go on. To avoid the snow-filled roadside ditches, we stick to the narrow verge. Here, melted runoff has frozen into patches of slippery, rutted ice and, to avoid falling, I find myself walking as I have seen all Muscovites walk in winter: I hardly lift my feet, almost slide them along the surface, balance at each step, and tread heavily without slackening pace. I have a theory that so much ice and snow during many months of the year ultimately affect the gait and posture of every Muscovite.

Once, when I was fairly new to the city, I was striding along a street, dressed like any other citizen in heavy coat and fur hat. A stranger walking beside me looked up and addressed me in accented English. "How do you like our Moscow?" he asked affably. "How did you know me for a foreigner?" I countered in Russian. "By your walk," he said. I was loping along in my typical New Yorker's fashion.

Now I walk as Muscovites do. My wife and I tramp on beside the roadway until we find a suitable spot to don skis and slip into the woods. As soon as we leave the highway, with its intermittent whir of passing cars, and lose sight of the apartment houses in the distance behind us, the city ceases to exist for us. A hush envelops the woods. Pines and spruce stand out green against the snow, and clumps of tall birches form sun-dappled walls. A few icicles on barren, black larch branches glint yellow in the sun.

When a Muscovite speaks of skiing, he usually means cross-country skiing. (There are two ski-jumps on the Lenin Hills in front of Moscow University, but to find ski slopes one must travel more than 150 miles to the Valdai Hills north of Moscow.) Now, in the silent woods we glide along undulating paths that weave in and out among the trees. There are a few trails left by skiers who preceded us, but we encounter only one or two fellow enthusiasts. We move in a blessed silence, immersed in the forest.

The whisper of the wind through snow-laden branches conjures up an image of a jingling *troika* coming through the woods. Enchanted, I daydream about these traditional Russian sleighs which have all but disappeared. One of the Moscow parks offers *troika* rides for foreign visitors during the winter tourist festival, early January snow permitting; and since 1957 there have been *troika* races every February at the Hippodrome

In winter two hardy Muscovites (below) refuse to let the depth of snow deter them from having a park-bench conversation. Later, after a thaw (right), a woman takes up a similar perch to read a book and keep her feet warm and dry.

racecourse near Begovaya Street. Like most Muscovites, however, I have seen genuine *troikas* only on the cinema screen; but I once heard the tinkle of a woman's necklace that had been made from beaten silver ornaments that long ago decorated a *troika* harness. The paper-thin silver wafers, each no larger than my smallest fingernail, gave off such a delicate rustle that it seemed to me the original harness must have sounded like a fairy tambourine—fit music for these snow-decked woods.

When we return to our apartment after our skiing expedition, stamping the snow from our shoes and brushing it from our jackets, we are grateful for the warmth. The door is padded and our double windows are sealed to keep out the chill as much as possible. Most Moscow housewives use the sill between the inner and outer panes to store jars of vegetables that have been pickled or salted for the winter: cucumbers, tomatoes, eggplant, sauerkraut with chopped apples and carrots. We, however, have sealed both frames tightly with strips of tape to keep the apartment snug.

Aglow after our day outdoors, we vow to repeat the excursion the following weekend. Next week, however, the snow is again grey and melting, the sky overcast, and the chill in the air is sullen. At such times I wonder

whether memory is playing tricks on me; whether the winter days of years past were cleaner, more brisk; and whether I have blotted out all recollection of bleak periods. Surely there were some. But Moscow friends confirm that the city's weather has changed significantly over the decades. Seated elbow to elbow around a crowded kitchen table, we speculate about it over many glasses of steaming tea. They mourn the change. Some superstitious Muscovites, they tell me, blame the warmer winters on everything from space launchings to nuclear tests.

My own theory is that Moscow is experiencing the same phenomenon that has affected most large cities: haze—generated by urban heat, soot and dust—forms an insulating blanket over the city. A meteorologist who published a study of Moscow in the mid-1960s compared records compiled in the city's centre and outskirts, and found that on many days the centre was warmer than the outskirts by as much as 10°F. The increase in temperature—a direct result of urban heating—was equivalent to moving the city nearly 200 miles south of its present latitude. Every few years, however, a hard winter interrupts this warming trend. In the winter of 1975-76, for example, temperatures fell to minus 22°F. In the opinion of my Muscovite friends that was a vintage year.

During the winter months Muscovites satisfy their cravings for greenery by raising plants indoors. At the markets, peasants sell bulbs, seeds and young plants. Many windows display touches of green, and at street level blooming plants are frequently arranged like trophies, curtains draped behind them so as to set them off. In recent years, also, the Japanese art of flower arrangement has become a fad.

At the beginning of March, when the city is still in the grip of winter, queues of men form outside Moscow's flower shops. They herald the approach of International Women's Day, one of the Soviet Union's official holidays, which falls on the eighth day of the month. It is a political occasion, marked by speeches in factories and offices, by awards and tributes to leading women workers, and by long newspaper articles about the role of women; but to me it seems more like a combination of St. Valentine's Day and Mother's Day.

The women get a half day off, husbands and children do the housework, and every woman expects to be given at least one flower. Each man queueing at the flower shops hopes to buy a cellophane-wrapped carnation or mimosa or, if he is particularly lucky, a rose or a tulip. Many will be disappointed, for hot-house production of cut flowers lags far behind demand. Each flower is therefore cherished. Several times—and not only in winter—I have seen a young man walk on stage at a Moscow theatre and present a singer or actress with a single, cellophane-wrapped flower in lieu of a bouquet. The demand for flowers continues into spring. In May, my wife, visiting one of the markets, saw a crowd surrounding a peasant just arrived from the country, his arms filled with marsh marigolds, his hipboots

Although most keen gardeners in Moscow must settle for a window box in their flat, this market stall selling flower seeds still does a busy trade. Customers get the seeds only, not what at first glance appear to be seed packets: actually cards handpainted by the stall's owner to show buyers what blossoms they can expect.

still wet. He had no time to set up his stall or even make change. The buyers besieged him.

For many years Georgians and Azerbaidzhani from sub-tropical parts of the Caucasus used to exploit the Muscovites' insatiable demand for flowers. They flew to Moscow with suitcases crammed with out-of-season blooms—sometimes reserving an extra seat for the suitcases—and returned with pockets stuffed with roubles. In 1974, campaigns against profiteers put a stop to this lucrative trade, but other sharp businessmen filled the breach. During the winter and spring shortages, hawkers demand four or five times the low government price for flowers, and get their price.

The harbingers of spring are the thud of snow being shovelled from roofs and the shattering of icicles as they fall to the street. High up on the slanting, metal roofs workmen clamber perilously, loosening the snow that has accumulated during winter and sending chunks sliding over the edges of the buildings on to the pavements below. Sometimes the men lash themselves to chimneys with safety ropes, sometimes they simply balance precariously on the steeply sloping roofs. Pedestrians, accustomed to the annual clean-up, step unconcernedly around barriers on the pavement while snow and ice crash down on the roped-off walks.

This rooftop activity is merely the forerunner of the real spring cleaning, which comes on Saturday in the week of Lenin's birthday, April 22. The entire city participates in what is called a *Subbotnik*, a Saturday of voluntary work. Factory workers put in a full day's labour on what is normally a half day and contribute the day's pay to funds for public works—factory projects, such as construction of a summer camp for children of the employees, and national projects, such as the building of a national cancer research centre. White-collar workers, housewives and youngsters spruce up the city's parks, playgrounds and courtyards. The *Subbotnik* tradition goes back to the Civil War days of 1919, when Moscow railway depot workers volunteered to work on a holiday as a contribution to the Revolution. Lenin hailed the precedent; and the next year, when the practice spread nationwide, himself participated by helping to load logs.

By chance that was the same job assigned to me when I took part in a *Subbotnik* in the 1930s. The Metro was under construction and, because I could not pass up the opportunity to be able to say that I had had a hand in building it, I volunteered my labour. The group I joined went down the shaft of the Dzerzhinsky Square station, then nearing completion. When we got to our allotted position, a brawny foreman looked us over and shook his head. Either we looked to be a puny lot or he did not know what to do with us. Finally he directed us to haul logs and pit props to one side of the tunnel, and to stack them there. We laboured mightily for several hours, getting in the way of other workers, tripping over obstacles, and becoming completely winded. I do not think we accomplished much, but the foreman thanked us for our efforts and, when we returned to the surface—blinking, dirty and with aching muscles—I felt a sense of pride.

During my most recent stay, I went to see the annual *Subbotnik* at Watch Factory No. 2, in a new area of light industry and large apartment buildings. The morning started with brief pep talks and awards to "outstanding workers of the year", but otherwise it seemed an ordinary working day for the 800 women employed in the assembly shop. Outside, however, ignoring a light drizzle, office workers, local residents and schoolchildren were swarming across the factory grounds and the streets, clearing rubbish, weeding, planting trees and whitewashing fences. There was a good deal of merriment around the kiosks selling ice cream and *chebureki*—steaming hot Georgian meat pasties. A beer stand did a lively trade, but the sale of hard liquor was forbidden that weekend.

Although the *Subbotnik* work is officially proclaimed to be voluntary, one of the amateur gardeners confided that, if he failed to turn out, he would never hear the end of it from trade union and party officials as well as some of his fellow employees. When I left the factory grounds, he was cajoling one of the prettier of the female *Subbotnik* gardeners into joining him that evening at a dance to be held at the watch factory. I did not attend the festivities; I went instead on a sentimental journey by Metro. My destination: Dzerzhinsky Square station. After all, I had helped build it.

Spring-cleaning continues throughout the week between the *Subbotnik* and May Day. Railings and park benches are painted, courtyards swept; street cleaners hose down the streets to remove the last of the winter grime, even though a snow flurry may yet dust the city again. Housewives strip away the cotton padding and paper tapes that sealed their windows all winter long, and scrub the panes. Janitors lend buckets to motorists who want to wash their cars. The motorists are not simply taking pride in a prized possession: city regulations bar dirty cars from the streets—in fact, vehicles entering Moscow are sometimes turned back at the city limits because they are mudstained. The regulation is never more strictly enforced than around May Day. The whole city gleams.

Red bunting and banners bearing May Day slogans go up all over town. Rosettes decorate the lamp posts on some streets, sprays of red flags festoon them on others. As part of the holiday illuminations, work crews string rows of electric lights along the cornices of buildings. Finally, the portraits of the *Politburo* members—the Soviet inner cabinet—are mounted on the façades of buildings. The faces are familiar to all, but once or twice the appearance of a new face or the disappearance of a familiar one signals the rise or downfall of a member before the official announcement.

Most of Moscow never sees the May Day Demonstration in person. It is not a parade, viewed by crowds along the line of march. It is just what the word says, a demonstration—or, as an American correspondent once put

On a cold, dark winter afternoon, a writer works in the snug, pine-clad study of his Peredelkino dacha.

A Cosseted Village

A well-to-do or privileged Muscovite with a *dacha*—country house—in the woods outside Moscow can savour the passing seasons with special pleasure. Some *dachas* are built on land granted by the state to top executives or to people who win international prestige. There are *dacha* communities for high government officials and others for famous scientists or artists. One such colony is Peredelkino, built by Stalin to reward loyal writers. Boris Pasternak, author of *Doctor Zhivago*, lived here—and kept his beloved *dacha* even after falling from official favour. In Peredelkino, writers and editors enjoy a placid life in a birch and pine forest only 15 minutes by car from central Moscow.

Viewed through wide expanses of glass, the thick summer greenery outside becomes almost part of the décor of this sunroom in a Peredelkino dacha, where friends meet over tea to discuss literature and life.

Clapboard and a children's swing lend a New England flavour to this house.

Tucked away among a stand of tall pines, this dacha has a fairytale look.

Deep, fresh snow does not prevent the daily stroll, even with baby in pram.

A parent gives a child instruction in the finer points of snowman building.

it, the world's biggest television spectacular, with a cast of millions. Only about a thousand VIPs, invited to the grandstand in Red Square, are spectators at the event; the rest of Moscow's people either take part or watch the spectacle on television.

Early in the morning on May Day the centre of town within the Boulevard Ring is blocked off. While the select audience filter through this empty, cordoned area and pass through a series of eight or nine checkpoints at the approach to Red Square, the hundreds of thousands of marchers assemble beyond the Boulevard. Each person marches with his factory, office or school. The marchers carry banners, posters, portraits of *Politburo* members and forests of twigs decorated with paper flowers. The groups of marchers stand about, stopping to let the groups ahead move on, then break into a run to catch up. Slow rivulets of marchers at the outer Garden Ring merge into streams at the inner Boulevard Ring. They form a torrent as they converge down the radial streets leading on to the square, and become a turbulent sea of faces and waving banners as they pass through.

The marchers go through the quarter-mile-long square at a quick step, between chains of parade marshals separating the columns. They crane their heads for a momentary glimpse of the remote dignitaries waving from the balcony above the Lenin Mausoleum. From the marchers' point of view, it is as if the men on the balcony were the ones on display, the marchers a fast-moving audience. Then it is over for them; the marchers turn in their banners on the other side of the square and wend their way home to their families, who have been watching it all on television. Similar parades, reviewed by local dignitaries, are being staged simultaneously in every city and town in the Soviet Union. The mind boggles at the thought of the millions marching—and the few thousand that go to watch them.

The evening of May Day is given over to the *gulyan'ye*, a word that defies exact translation. Fete? Too pretentious. Carnival? You will find no riotous revelry here. Promenade? That comes closest in meaning but it is too stiff and formal. No, *gulyan'ye* it must remain; a tradition that has its roots in the strolling and singing on Russian village greens, and which has been transplanted to the city's streets and squares.

During the *gulyan'ye* everyone is out at popular points throughout Moscow to see the illuminations and watch the fireworks displays. The fireworks go up from about a dozen squares scattered about town and, because of the wide boulevards that provide an unobstructed view of the night sky, they are visible from every part of the city. Muscovites have become rather blasé about the displays; for, in addition to May Day, there are fireworks on Army-Navy Day in February, VE-Day in May, a separate Navy Day in July, Air Force Day in August, Armoured Forces Day in September, the anniversary of the Revolution in November, Artillery and Missile Forces Day later in November, and one or two others. There are other occasions that do not merit fireworks, some of which I have already

Smiling apprehensively—perhaps because her friend is looking at the result—a woman checks her weight in Gorky Amusement Park. Having an attendant to operate public scales may seem a waste of manpower; but for the old man who does the job, the few roubles he earns are a welcome supplement to his state pension.

mentioned. When I add that there are also Railwayman's Day, Miner's Day, Teacher's Day, Farmer's Day, and a whole host of other "days", it is apparent that the Soviet calendar is jampacked with ceremonies that include propaganda, speeches and meetings.

But May Day is special, not least because it ushers in spring after the long winter. For the Slavic tribes in pagan times, May Day was the feast of Yarilo the Sun God. Warily, the Muscovites at the *gulyan'ye* cling to dark, heavy winter coats, in case the weather turns cold again. But spring *is* in the air, and the crowds reflect it in their mood. They flock to eight- and ten-lane lower Gorky Street, which is closed to traffic for the occasion; and when it grows dark, they fill it from pavement to pavement for three-quarters of a mile, milling about and admiring the decorations.

The young flirt and, here and there, groups of four or five walk arm in arm, singing. ("Careful, citizens!" admonishes a jostled father with a child perched on his shoulders.) On the river embankment beneath the university heights, Muscovites pour out of the Metro station in a steady stream and spread out along the hilly, grassy walks beside the river, seeking boulders and tree stumps on which to sit while watching the fireworks and the throng. Muscovites are usually prudish about public displays of affection, but I notice that some young couples have their arms round each other's waists, and one or two young men strum guitars as they stroll. Pairs of teenage girls giggle at the attentions of the boys following them. Ten- and 11-year-olds scurry through the crowd, shouting to each other. It grows dark. When the fireworks go up, faces are bathed in pink or purple or golden light, and the youngsters cheer at each pinwheel or starburst.

Spring brings out club cyclists whizzing Indian-file alongside traffic on the Garden Ring, and pony-tailed girls jogging in blue track suits near the university. In the courtyards, motorists lift their cars off storage blocks and remove protective tarpaulins. Along the boulevards, faint green tints the damp earth, and pruned and pollarded trees (the cut twigs are used to make brooms for sweeping the streets) burst into pale bud. Migrant birds return, and the numerous descendants of the pigeons that Nikita Khrushchev introduced to Moscow during the 1957 youth festival, to symbolize peace, coo in the eaves. Wheeled carts selling *kvas*, a type of beer made from fermented bread, return to street corners. Windows reflect light from the sun; and buildings whose colour I would have called "indeterminate" in winter now appear in their true pastel tones: pale cream, stucco grey, pink. A few are painted in the light blues and greens that soften the appearance of so many Russian towns.

The Orthodox Easter often falls around May Day, and then even irreligious Muscovites shop at the peasant market stalls for *kulich*, the traditional Easter buns, and make *paskha*, a delicacy of sweetened cheese curds and raisins. The peasant women display their winter handiwork:

heaps of wooden Easter eggs painted in bright reds, greens and yellows, all bearing simple motifs—a rooster, say, or a church—and often the Cyrillic initials *XB* for the Old Church Slavonic words *Khristos voskresse*, "Christ has risen".

The spring days of timid sun are interspersed with heavy, chill rain; but the weather is warm enough for Muscovites to start shedding their drab winter clothing. The children who in winter looked like stuffed bears turn out to have legs after all. Bright raincoats and coloured umbrellas, a welcome change from the customary black and grey of earlier times, dot the busy crowds of shoppers dodging puddles on lower Petrovka and Kuznetsky Most. May is hardly ended when the graduating students of secondary schools take over Red Square for a night-long *gulyan'ye* before they begin the round of competitive exams for admission to universities and technical institutes.

And suddenly Moscow's summer has begun.

Theatres shut down. Families start the exodus to country *dachas* in the woods near the beaches along the Moscow River. Busloads of children set off for summer camps operated by the Young Pioneers organization, the Communist equivalent of Boy and Girl Scouts. The city moves outdoors to parks and courtyards. It is too soon for youngsters to plunge into Moscow's cold ponds and swimming holes, but fishermen line the river embankment. Ferris wheels and loop-the-loops open in the amusement parks. Plaster statues, some with broken arms, stand out against the greenery in the 16 Parks of Culture and Rest. Couples hire rowing boats on the park ponds, and canoeists paddle kayaks down the river.

The city becomes dusty and hot. Summer motorists add to the traffic and earn the wrath of taxi drivers, who blame them for the hazards of city driving—although, when I see the taxicabs dodging from lane to lane and accelerating to beat red lights, I know the blame is not all one-sided. Not until 1975 was the city speed limit reduced from 50 miles an hour to 35.

Sunday gardeners stake out tiny plots just outside the city limits and move their gardening tools into makeshift sheds amid a crazy network of rude fences. Muscovites exhibit an intense passion for gardening. Once, passing a high-rise apartment building at midnight, I saw a man in pyjamas wielding a garden hose from his second-storey balcony to water a patch of grass and flowers below him, in front of the ten-storey building. It was not his patch, mind you; just a little pocket of greenery to gladden passers-by.

On park benches, along the boulevards and in the courtyards, elderly pensioners and youngsters play chess, while others slap down dominoes with triumphant gestures. After work, the men chat at street-corner beer stands and women gather in the courtyards, contributing to the city's relaxed, shirt-sleeved atmosphere. Moscow is full of surprises when its life is laid bare to the sunlight.

One of the surprises I experienced upon returning to Moscow in the 1970s was the sight of dogs being walked during the long summer evenings. I cannot recall having seen dogs in Moscow in the 1930s, when food was scarce and it was hard to feed them. In the 1950s the few I saw were practical, watchdog breeds. But in the seventies Muscovites walked show dog breeds, lap dogs, hunting dogs, a few St. Bernards and wolfhounds, and just plain dogs. My family used to visit the outdoor pet market near Taganka Square, a gathering place for dog lovers. There you were apt to see a puppy peeping out from between its seller's coat lapels, or a youngster offering a jar of guppies, or cages of parrots and canaries.

Most of the Muscovites' summer activities are outdoor ones; but that does not mean they must leave town to find empty spaces. My wife discovered a large city park where, to our delight, the grass grew high and nightingales sang in the evening. My family used to pursue a favourite Moscow summer occupation: mushroom-hunting in the woods. Few things are more welcome to the Russian palate than mushrooms—eaten raw, pickled, salted, dried or broiled. And there are few aspects of nature lore more intriguing than the finding and identifying of the many varieties of edible fungi that grow in and around Moscow.

Autumn brings abundance to the peasant markets and a quickening of pace as Muscovites prepare for the long winter. At the colourful indoor markets, peasants in white aprons and oversleeves preside over heaps of tomatoes, cabbages, apples, pears, berries and flowers. The peasant woman traders lure you with tempting displays of food and flowers, chat about varieties, invite you to sample their products and wish you good health. You are likely to hear not only dissertations on the merits of the produce of different regions, but also the life stories of the traders and their family concerns. Yellow and green melons are stacked in mounds—connoisseurs place them to their ears, shake them and listen to gauge their ripeness and quality. Hawkers wear strings of dried mushrooms or onions draped around their necks and stretching to their knees. Housewives flock to the markets, on the sound principle that one must buy while the supply lasts. In this northern clime the bounty is short-lived. It is now that the housewives will pickle, dry, salt and can the excess vegetables, and store them away for the winter when supplies will be scarce.

Autumn brings a jam of returning holiday-makers at airports and railway stations. Aeroflot, the national airline, has been in the habit of scheduling every aeroplane at its disposal; inevitably, some of the aircraft develop mechanical faults, are withdrawn from service, and the schedule breaks down. When flights are delayed, sometimes for days, passengers in transit simply sit it out at the airports. In 1973, 10,000 passengers at one time were stranded at Moscow's Domodedovo Airport during a three-day interruption of scheduled autumn flights to the Far East. Many slept in the woods around the airport. A massive scandal ensued, and Aeroflot promised to mend its ways.

Nevertheless, early autumn still finds airports and railway waiting rooms overflowing. Some of the travellers are students returning from summer camps where they have helped on farms or construction projects. They wear green jackets with the prized insignia showing that they have so served. The city bustles. Road repairs are carried out, day and night, in preparation for the winter frosts. There is talk of weather and crops, for Muscovites remember the disastrous droughts of 1972 and 1975 when grain had to be imported from the United States and Canada. In 1972 the drought was so bad that a 9,000-acre peat bog 80 miles away caught fire, and for days the city dwellers' eyes smarted from the smoke. There is some resentment of the travellers who pass through the city and use the opportunity to shop for food in competition with Muscovites, but this attitude is tempered by a certain amount of head-shaking sympathy for travellers from parts of the country where supplies are poor.

The warm, sunny autumn weather soon gives way to raw, cold rainy days; the yellow leaves on the birch trees drop almost overnight. Theatres re-open, restaurants fill up, lines form in front of the better cafés each evening. Unlike the old-time peasants, who virtually hibernated near their tiled or clay stoves during the cold months, Muscovites find their pulses quickening when the first frosts glaze the city. On November 7 they celebrate the anniversary of the Revolution—a ceremony that is a re-run of May Day with the addition of a military parade. The weather is cold, clammy, overcast; flocks of noisy crows circle over the Kremlin. Soon afterwards the first snow drifts down. Moscow bundles up for the long winter. The cycle of the seasons is complete.

Winter's Zestful Pleasures

PHOTOGRAPHS BY DICK ROWAN

Leaning back on a sled improvised from a piece of cardboard, a father and daughter glide down a length of Gorky Park's 120,000 square yards of ice-slide.

During the four or five months each year that Moscow is blanketed with snow, outdoor leisure activities continue unabated. For a dedicated few, winter sports are a serious matter, involving training in gymnasiums and sports palaces; and there is a hardy minority who relish bathing in the frozen Moscow River. But most Muscovite pleasures are less rigorous: thousands enjoy escaping from centrally heated buildings into the crisp cold of city parks, where they can skate on ponds or simply slide on the miles of specially flooded paths (above). Many go cross-country skiing in the birch and pine forests fringing the city limits. Others enjoy the more placid sport of ice-fishing, while there are those who prefer merely to wrap up well in warm clothes and watch harness racing at the Hippodrome, where the horses run all the year round.

A skier leaps towards Moscow's skyline—with the Luzhniki Stadium directly ahead in the distance. This jump is one of two in Moscow, both on the Lenin Hills.

Weaving determinedly, a six-year-old slalomer tries to negotiate an obstacle.

A Rage for Skiing

Skiing is the special delight of Muscovites of all ages. The first heavy snowfalls bring out a motley set of devotees—from children (above) to the few accomplished sportsmen who defy gravity on the city's ski-jumps (opposite). But most Muscovites are devoted to their traditional cross-country skiing over the relatively flat terrain surrounding the city.

Fishing in Icy Waters

Many Muscovites while away winter afternoons ice-fishing for perch, pike or ruff in frozen ponds and rivers. The sport is simple, requiring only a hole in the ice, a small rod and line, patience—and perhaps a bottle of vodka to help ward off the cold. More than most forms of angling, ice-fishing is a contemplative man's recreation. After the fisherman has drilled his hole with an auger, he has little to do but wait until a tug on the line signals a bite.

Like little figures in a Breughel snow scene, fishermen hunch patiently over holes bored in an ice-covered branch of the Moscow River within the city limits.

In the lavishly decorated grandstand that dates back to Czarist times, fur-hatted devotees discuss form between races at the Moscow Hippodrome.

A Frigid Day at the Races

Moscow's horse racing centre is the Hippodrome, on Begovaya Street, in the north-west of the city. Its stables house more than 500 horses. Meetings are held three days a week in all seasons, but only troika and harness races are run during winter. Betting is run by the state, although private bookies also operate with the tacit consent of the course authorities. The Hippodrome's revenues subsidize leading Moscow theatres, including the Bolshoi.

Perched on fragile-looking sulkies, crash-helmeted jockeys jostle for position as their horses dash at a fast trot down a snowy straight during a harness race.

A white-haired athlete walks briskly past muffled observers in Gorky Park.

Connoisseurs of Cold

Some of Moscow's citizens are so fond of winter that they celebrate it by taking off their clothes. Members of this masochistic minority have their own nickname ("walruses") and their own meeting places (holes cut in the Moscow River), where they traditionally gather for a dip every New Year's Day. Others are content to take constitutionals in the city's parks.

With ascetic dedication to physical fitness, a muscular midwinter swimmer hauls himself out of a hole cut through the thick ice of the frozen Moscow River.

5
What Makes the City Tick?

In the largest hall of the Great Kremlin Palace, the Supreme Soviet of the U.S.S.R.—the "parliament" or legislative assembly of the Soviet Union—sits in session. The chamber, reconstructed in 1934 from two adjacent 19th-Century halls, can accommodate 2,500 people.

Generations of Russians have echoed the cry of Irina in Chekhov's *Three Sisters*: "To Moscow! To Moscow!" As in Chekhov's day, Russians come here to escape the limitations of provincial life; but nowadays they also come to build careers in the capital's huge political and administrative bureaucracies. At the same time, Moscow is the country's greatest industrial centre. Most of all, however, Russians are drawn to Moscow because, as the capital, it is favoured above all other Soviet cities. It has *more* of everything. Life here is better than anywhere else in the Soviet Union.

Thus, to live in Moscow is a privilege; and the officially registered citizen of Moscow recognizes that he or she is a very lucky individual in comparison with other Soviet citizens. I have met only one Muscovite, something of an eccentric, who would rather live in a village than in Moscow. Much to my envy, he spends a great part of the year amid mountain scenery; but even he will not give up his precious legal residence as a Muscovite, and he returns periodically to the city. There are some, of course, who leave Moscow of their own free will—lured by high pay and the call of adventure to new towns in Siberia or cotton-rich Central Asia; but they are very few. On the other hand, there is no lack of people seeking to move to Moscow.

The days of mass migration to the capital, such as I witnessed in the 1930s, are, however, over. Government regulations have seen to that. Moreover, Moscow is still plagued by a scarcity of housing. Even if new accommodation could be built, there are limits to how much the city can conveniently grow. Consequently, although Moscow suffers from a labour shortage, it is trying to prevent any further increase in population, even dispersing some of its industry outside the city to restrict growth.

But with the lure of Moscow so strong, some Russians will do anything to live there. They know that they will need police permission (all Soviet citizens must register with the police, wherever they live), a place to settle and a job; and, since each of the three requirements depends on the other two, that the chance of obtaining them is a bit like a dog chasing its tail. But they try. One dodge is to move to the city as a dependant or relative of a Moscow resident. I have heard of people entering into marriages of convenience—sometime even for a steep cash price—solely for the purpose of acquiring official status as Muscovites.

A lucky few are invited to Moscow by a factory or some other organization that needs their services. They fall mostly into two categories: brilliant young university graduates or specialists, and those who are willing to accept grubby, ill-paid jobs that long-time Moscow residents, with many choices in a bottomless labour market, disdain. This is not to say that they must remain at a menial job forever; they move up to better things as soon as they can. Country girls, who used to seek employment as housemaids when I first came to Moscow, now hire themselves out as hospital attendants, house painters, plasterers, restaurant dishwashers—jobs that often come with dormitory accommodation. I have also met Volga Tatars (and other newcomers to Moscow) who work as refuse collectors, janitors, car-park attendants and unskilled factory labourers.

To digress for a moment, I would like to point to the scarcity of white-collar workers in Moscow: secretaries, typists, clerks, draughtsmen. Presumably, people from the hinterlands could help fill such a void; but in Russia's proletarian society, the job emphasis remains steadfastly on industry and construction, and this means that executives spend 40 per cent of their time doing office chores because of the lack of assistants. In 1974 the country had only seven secretarial schools, of which two were in Moscow. Typists were badly paid, stenographers few, and the position of secretary did not even merit a listing in the Soviet handbook of jobs and qualifications. A shortage of office equipment made the problem worse: in 1975 the country's home production met only one-fifth of the estimated annual need for typewriters; and many a secretary had to make do with a table and a straight-backed wooden seat instead of a proper desk and chair.

When the daughter of an acquaintance of mine chose to go to secretarial school it struck me as such a novelty that I wrote an article on the subject for an American newspaper, remarking that some day sculptors might have to redesign the statue that stands above the entrance to Moscow's Exhibition of National Economic Achievements. In the minds of millions it symbolizes the Soviet Union—it depicts a brawny worker holding a hammer, and a farm woman with a sickle and sheaf of grain. The new version would make room in the ensemble for a secretary at her typewriter. But that day is still a long way off.

Whatever their job, those lucky enough to call Moscow home are employed by the state either directly or indirectly. And since practically every adult Muscovite holds a job of some kind (only about 3 per cent of the women are full-time mothers and housewives), this means that Moscow is, in a manner of speaking, a one-company town. The paternalistic employer provides the worker with a wide range of services, from nurseries and kindergartens to theatre tickets and vacations. The employer may even intercede with the local housing authorities—not always successfully—on behalf of an employee who is in dire need of a room or apartment. In addition, many firms and organizations sponsor housing construction co-operatives in which the more highly paid employees invest to buy an apartment with the help of a 10-year, 2 per cent state bank loan.

A wild goose flies through the smoky haze hanging over an industrial suburb of Moscow. Government policy now is to move such plants away to satellite towns.

The employer-employee relationship is furthered by the trade union. Russian trade unions bear little resemblance to their Western counterparts. They are essentially company unions. To begin with, they do not strike—although strikes are not specifically forbidden by law. I am reminded of an incident involving my wife and myself. We were standing late one evening outside the Hotel Rossia—where I think Moscow's most independent taxi drivers congregate—trying vainly to get a cab. A dozen taxis were lined up, but the drivers apparently had already met their prescribed quota of earnings for the day; and although their shift was not over, they had no inclination to accept another fare. They were standing about, smoking and chatting. We asked driver after driver whether his cab was available, but one after another they turned their backs, shrugged and walked away. It was beginning to look hopeless, when my wife had an inspiration. She turned to one of the drivers and said innocently: "Is this a strike? I didn't know there were strikes in the Soviet Union." The driver was startled. He stared at us briefly, stepped to the door of his cab, opened the door and gestured for us to enter.

Instead of confronting the employer on behalf of the workers, the Soviet trade union abets him in campaigns to increase production, runs the welfare and social security systems and, together with the employer and the Party, it distributes rewards and patronage. In collaboration with employers, the unions maintain clubs, sports grounds, gymnasiums, and swimming pools; they organize hobby groups, amateur arts circles, classes in every subject from Art to Zoology, excursions to museums and historic towns, and co-operatives to build summer cottages. They allocate space in sanatoriums, rest homes, summer camps and resorts, often subsidizing part of the vacation cost. They distribute large numbers of theatre tickets and help employees to secure out-of-town summer garden plots. They administer the retirement pension system, issue health insurance benefits and direct the factory safety programmes.

Not surprisingly, the Muscovite's life revolves around his place of employment. Moscow's largest establishments and industries constitute self-sufficient communities, with their own clubhouses, bookshops, newspaper stands, hairdressers, beauty parlours, clinics, pharmacies, laundries, shoe- and watch-repair stands, lecture halls, excursion bureaux, photography studios, cafeterias. The list of facilities seems endless.

The employee may even depend upon employer and union to alleviate the shortages that from time to time still plague Moscow or to ease his lot in other ways. During the 1972 drought when potatoes—so basic to the Soviet diet—were scarce, some managers sent lorries all the way to Belorussia, a Western Soviet region where the harvest was good, to bring back supplies for sale to their employees. Because shops are still scarce in the newer residential areas of the city, the employers try to provide some shopping facilities at places of work.

The employer also manages the distribution of some prized, rare luxuries, such as motor cars, to key personnel. The waiting lists for the purchase of an automobile may be several years long, but a share of the country's production is assigned to large or influential employers, to be allocated as awards to executives and outstanding performers. The employer can then grant a precious priority to purchase a car—at the full price—without the buyer having to sweat out the long waiting list. Employers and unions also distribute the equally prized tickets for group tours abroad—mostly to the East European countries, but occasionally to the West. If seats at some theatres are at a premium, the employer uses his influence to obtain some. Often I have watched representatives of a powerful political or government agency—or sometimes a factory—walk to the head of the queue at a theatre box office, present a paper, and receive a fistful of tickets. They were exercising the *bronya*, the right to reserve a certain number of seats.

Hundreds of such threads tie employee to employer, with the union in between, in a symbiotic body that is called "the collective". Community activities that in the West focus around one's place of residence—from the sports society to civil defence—are concentrated here at one's place of employment. Each Party member is assigned to a unit at his factory, rather than to a unit in his neighbourhood. In the May Day and November 7 demonstrations every individual marches in the employing organization's column. Sports teams, organized into local and national leagues, are supported by employers and trade unions. The athletes get factory sinecures, as in the United States they get college scholarships.

The factory is also the centre for political activity. Here is where Khrushchev's unprinted speech about Stalin was read out to the public, and here lecturers rehash major *Pravda* editorials and party and government declarations. Here are held the more-or-less compulsory courses in current events, Party history, and economics. And then there are the meetings—from the "five-minute" planning sessions that run on for more than half an hour to the ritual pep talks and lengthy harangues during or after work. I remember seeing a Russian film that had a scenario devoted entirely to a Party committee meeting at a factory; the film lasted two hours and was a breathtaking exposé of the practice of faking plan fulfilment in order to obtain bonuses.

Although workers in heavy industry and defence projects receive higher wages and better facilities than those in consumer-goods industries, the grades, ratings and salary ranges of Moscow employees—as throughout the Soviet Union—are standard within each occupation. Pay, however, depends not merely on one's job or grade, but also on piece work, and even more on plan fulfilment by the entire shop or factory.

It seems to me that, in spite of the constant propaganda exhorting the workers to achieve higher output, few strive hard to exceed work quotas—

Coupled with the legend "The Achievement of the Presnya Workers", this huge mural on a building in Moscow's Krasnaya Presnya district reminds passers-by of the local factory workers who played a major role in the armed uprising against Czarism in the 1905 Revolution.

and with good reason. It is common knowledge that as soon as work quotas are exceeded, they are raised, and this knowledge acts as a deterrent to the zealous. On the other hand, every employee wants the shop, factory or office to fulfil its monthly plan, since bonuses, which are a regular part of the earnings of most workers, depend on that achievement.

The need to meet monthly production goals creates a peculiar work rhythm. Partly because of inefficient supply and partly because of the habit to which a monthly working cycle accustoms people, the early portion of the month is spent in gathering materials and parts, and in gearing up, and the rest is a frantic rush to meet the prescribed quota. *Shturmovshchina*, "taking by storm", is the name given to this accelerating pace. Although overtime is ostensibly forbidden, workers are sometimes called upon to put in extra hours at the end of the month in order to achieve production goals. Since monetary compensation for overtime would disclose the unsanctioned extra hours and disrupt the factory's budget, the workers are granted days off at the beginning of the next month in lieu of extra pay. Consequently, work starts at a crawl, and the cycle begins again.

Offices have their own production goals, with quotas of paper work to be fulfilled; even political agencies and trade unions make up monthly quotas of "measures" to be taken—the number of lectures to be delivered, for example. Shops have quarterly and annual sales quotas. Some Muscovites believe that shop staffs make extra efforts to obtain desirable goods at the end of the year, when they may be in jeopardy of falling short of their sales quotas for the year.

I myself think there is a different reason why the shops get more goods at the close of the year: to foster a festive atmosphere on the eve of the New Year holiday. Shops are also better stocked before May Day and November 7, and on special political occasions, such as the Party Congress, which is held every five years. The mania for dressing up the city on such occasions is carried to the extreme of hastily tearing down old buildings and laying out squares and gardens in their place. This happened when President Nixon visited Moscow in 1972. Muscovites look forward to important political events that are accompanied by an improvement in the supply of goods in the shops.

The way in which the Soviet economy is run contributes directly to the drab appearance of Moscow's shops. The city has two showcase shopping districts, Gorky Street and Kalinin Prospekt, as well as a few scattered speciality shops that attempt to display goods attractively. By comparison with the department stores of Western cities, however, even Moscow's best seem shabby. Clothing, furniture and other durables are mostly low in quality, old-fashioned in design, high in price and limited in variety. One reason is that manufacturers go on turning out low-grade, outmoded or already overstocked items because it is easier to fulfil the production plan

ПОДВИГ
ПРЕСНЕНСКИХ
РАБОЧИХ

if they do not take the time to modernize or improve the product but continue to make the same item year after year.

In other words, Moscow has a planned economy, but that does not make it a well-planned one, at least insofar as consumer goods are concerned. The manufacturers' neglect of quality and demand is aggravated by inefficient distribution. Once when I went in search of a broom, I found plenty of broom brushes, but no broom handles. After scouring the shops, I consulted a friend. "That's strange," he said, "there were plenty of broom handles last month." "Were there any broom brushes then?" I asked him. "Come to think of it, no." I never did find my broom handle.

There was a time when Muscovites accepted whatever goods they could get. Now, however, they cast about constantly in search of quality, snatching up every attractive item. When especially desirable commodities are put on sale at department stores, queues form all the way to the back stairs. I have seen those stairs packed as solid as a New York subway train at rush-hour. Let a scarce item be placed on the counters unexpectedly, and you will be caught in a riptide of shoppers, shoving with the same fierce determination that New Yorkers exhibit at a bargain-basement sale.

Except that this is not a sale; the Muscovite does not look for a bargain. The New Yorker says, "I can get it for you wholesale". The Muscovite who wants to boast that he can do you a favour says, "I can get it for you". I remember that, in 1974, 60 Moscow stores for the first time held spring sales, to clear out overstocked items. When I toured the stores, I found apathetic shoppers eyeing a small assortment of mostly unattractive leftover goods. There was no crush; in fact, there seemed to be fewer shoppers than usual. Some women were buying artificial silk scarves at half price, others were glancing idly at stacks of cheap handbags. But most of the shoppers ignored the undistinguished clothing and footwear. By contrast, there were queues in front of other shops selling fashionable garments and shoes at standard, high prices.

Muscovites are accustomed to stable, uniform, state-set prices—low for essentials such as bread, and for so-called cultural goods such as books and recordings; high for durables such as quality clothing and household furnishings; and extremely high for scarce luxuries such as motor cars. The high prices of some goods subsidize the low prices of necessities. Given low, subsidized rent, free health care and full employment for men and women, the better-paid Muscovites have roubles to spare, and they prowl the shops in search of desirable goods.

What do such Muscovites hope to buy? In the 1930s a pair of rubber galoshes was a prize find; today no one would be interested. In the 1940s wrist watches and good razor blades were sought after; now Soviet timepieces and electric shavers are plentiful in Moscow shops. In the 1950s the Muscovite might have wanted a Chinese fountain pen; nowadays he or she writes with a Soviet ballpoint. In the 1960s Muscovite couples

At the sprawling weekend pet bazaar on the city's outskirts, a formidable Great Dane dressed up in its show medals draws a concerned look from a hurrying little girl who clutches a puppy she has just bought. Although it is known as the Bird Market, stalls there sell cats, dogs, tropical fish and guinea pigs as well as birds, pet foods and other supplies.

hunted for good furniture (they still do); in the early 1970s they looked for scarce blue jeans, fashionably wide ties and women's pantsuits, some from East European countries. Muscovites searched for hi-fi sets, colour television and large refrigerators with freezer compartments, but rarely found them. There were people who aspired to buy a coloured lavatory bowl. And there were times when even flints for cigarette lighters were hard to come by.

Two categories of Muscovites are cushioned against the inadequacies of Moscow's retail shops: the *nomenklatura* and the foreigners. The *nomenklatura* is the Party's list of top-echelon positions—Party, governmental and economic—and of the persons holding these jobs. Moscow—with its concentration of Party agencies, ministries, news media, scientific laboratories, cultural institutions and defence establishments—probably has as high a proportion of officials and executives as New York and Washington combined; and these high ranking Russians enjoy some of the same perquisites as their American counterparts. Some have expense accounts, others travel in government limousines; but perhaps the most valued privilege of the *nomenklatura* is access to "closed" shops—like U.S. Army Post Exchange shops—which are reputedly well-stocked with goods at low prices. In addition, their children get into the best Moscow schools and have a very good chance of admission to the leading institutions of higher education. Moscow does not have country clubs, but the *nomenklatura* can relax in their summer homes at Black Sea resorts and in the best suburban *dachas* which, like the curtained, chauffeur-driven limousine, "go with the job". Highly placed writers, dancers, singers and actors share some of these perquisites.

Foreigners living in Moscow are similarly privileged. Correspondents, businessmen and embassy staffs are entitled to buy cars without waiting, and to buy them duty-free; to claim the best theatre tickets and to exercise priority in hotel and travel reservations; to have five- and six-room apartments; and to enjoy access to their own "closed" shops, the Beryozka chain, where foreign currency buys a wide variety of goods at prices comparable to or lower than prices abroad.

Curiously, some Westerners in Moscow, who regard their stay there as a hardship in spite of such special treatment, experience a kind of shock at the similar perquisites of the *nomenklatura.* They assume that Soviet society ought to be egalitarian on the Chinese pattern. It is not; but the gap between high and low, although considerable, is hardly as wide as it is in the West. And although I have frequently heard the city's citizens grumble about the troubles of the *un*privileged Moscow shopper, I sensed envy rather than resentment when they talked about the privileged. They took it for granted that the privileges went with the job. When I commented to an acquaintance on the luxuriousness of a curtained official limousine

At the meat counter of Moscow's Central Farmers' Market a customer makes her week's purchase of fatty pork. Peasants from collective farms in the surrounding countryside rent stalls in the modern, three-storey building where they sell—at competitive, rather than state-set prices—the fruits, vegetables, meat and dairy items that they produce on their private plots.

as it sped by through traffic, he responded: "Do you want our ministers to travel by bus?"

For the ordinary Muscovite, routine shopping is both arduous and time-consuming. The customer has to stand in line three times: once to select the goods, once to pay for the goods at the cashier's desk, and once to pick up the purchase. To obtain many categories of goods one must repeat the procedure in each different shop or department. For most Muscovites, shopping for food is an almost daily necessity, because even those with refrigerators have only small ones, and very few own cars in which to carry home several days' supplies. Consequently, shoppers make the rounds of the butcher shop, the dairy, the grocery, and so on—and at each stop there are the lines three times over. As a result, many Muscovites have their main meal—a three-course midday dinner—in the employee cafeterias at work, and settle for a simple supper at home. In the 1970s self-service shops were opened, but they were few and they suffered the drawback of a time-consuming procedure of checking packages or briefcases which the purchaser carried.

Although shopping entails a formidable waste of time, some experienced Muscovites find shortcuts. They know the standard goods, grades and prices, and the merest glance tells them what is being offered on a given day. If they decide to buy, they measure the line at the cashier's desk. If it is long, they employ the Moscow etiquette of queueing. "Who is last? I am behind you," the Muscovite says, thus establishing a place in line, and then proceeds to other departments before returning to claim the place. Couples or friends often share the shopping chores: one stands in line, while the other goes to another queue or reconnoitres the display counters. Many Muscovites have learned to run out during their lunch hour to choose goods and pay for them, then return after work to present the receipt and collect their purchases. In summer they patronize street stalls selling vegetables or dairy products, where they stand in line only once and pay the sales clerk who weighs and issues the goods.

Shopping for baked goods is a simple affair—and more enjoyable. I love the smell of the hearty Russian bread and the pleasure of choosing among the many wholesome varieties. In the early 1970s the bakeries introduced a more expensive, waxpaper-wrapped white loaf in the American style, complete with preservative to make it seem always fresh. Like most die-hard Muscovites, I prefer to walk along the rows of bins in the bakery, testing the freshness of the unwrapped varieties by using the flat side of the large forks that lie on the shelf for that purpose; enjoying the aromas, asking when the bakery will have Mozhaisk or Borodino or Yaroslavl or some other regional variety of bread, listening to the click of the cashier's abacus as she adds up the kopeks, hearing snatches of the day's gossip, and finally asking the assistant to slice one of the large loaves in half for a smaller portion. Because I invariably forget to bring a shopping bag, I usually walk out of the bakery with a half loaf of one kind under one arm, a half loaf of another variety under the other, and a roll or bun in each hand. This makes it all but impossible for me to fish for my apartment key when I get to my door.

At all Moscow shops the sales staff, caught between importunate buyers and erratic suppliers, can be notoriously rude. A customer can, however, tame an offending assistant by demanding the complaint book in which to inscribe a grievance, sometimes costing the assistant a dressing-down or deprivation of a bonus when the book is reviewed at a shop meeting. Usually, however, matters are settled with a spirited exchange of remarks in which the whole line of customers may join.

Once, in a neighbourhood bakery—near the central market, where peasants sell their produce and buy city goods—I saw a peasant woman press loaf after loaf with the flat of a fork. "Stale, stale, they're all stale!" she grumbled loudly.

"What are you complaining about? Who saved you from the fascists?" the buxom cashier shouted with glorious irrelevance.

"Fascists are fascists, but the bread is stale," the peasant woman insisted.

"Everybody working hard, and you complaining! It's good bread," the cashier went on.

"Nevertheless, it *is* stale!"

"But there *is* bread!" the cashier responded.

Finally, the peasant paid for her bread and turned to leave. As she got to the door she shouted back at the cashier: "And I tell you, it's stale!" She cast a withering glance at the other customers, and left.

"Probably buying it for her pigs, anyway," the cashier muttered defensively. She was referring to newspaper stories about the peasants' illegal

Colourful boxes of baby food and tins of milk indicate some effort to employ Western techniques of attractive packaging. But the sparse window display reflects the fact that Moscow remains a sellers' market in spite of increased availability of consumer goods.

practice of buying city bread for their livestock in lieu of scarce feed.

Finally the cashier called out to another assistant behind the bins. "Hey, Dusya, do you have any fresh bread there? Maybe we ought to put some in the bins."

She looked about, embarrassed yet self-righteous.

When Muscovites shopping for food do not find what they want in the state stores, they turn to the 30 peasant markets in Moscow. Here the collective farms sell that part of their produce not committed to the state, and the farmworkers offer meat and dairy products from their privately owned livestock and the crops from the personal garden plots that they tend in their spare time. The peasant markets supply about one-fifth of the city's meat, dairy products, fruit and vegetables. Prices depend on demand, and are usually higher—sometimes two to three times higher—than prices in state stores, but quality and variety are assured and there is always the chance of picking up off-season foods and unexpected items.

A Muscovite on the prowl for some special consumer item will go to the commission store, or secondhand shop, which offers the challenge of a treasure hunt. Here he may find such used goods as furniture, hi-fi sets, cameras and clothing, or even old gold, silver, cut glass and tableware. Many a foreigner has picked up antiques, bric-à-brac and samovars in the commission stores. The modern, electrically heated samovar is an unattractive, utilitarian type of kettle that few Muscovites use; but 19th-Century samovars are art objects, with pedigrees of maker, age and design. Foreigners have taken so many out of the country that the authorities now classify any article made before the Second World War—and not only samovars—as an antique, and a permit is required for its export.

Shopping for books can be another kind of adventure. They are in such demand that editions of hundreds of thousands sell out in a single day.

To make matters worse, books are not always reprinted if demand is high. I searched a dozen Moscow bookshops for a new volume by the poet Andrei Voznesensky, only to be told that it had been sold out before the 60,000 copies were officially released for sale. The poet himself could not get a spare copy. I tried Leningrad shops, also in vain. Finally I chanced upon a copy in a small Siberian town.

When a Moscow sales clerk brings out an armful of new titles to put them on the shelves, customers rush forward to grab them. Once I saw a clerk open a crate of books on the pavement in front of a shop on Kuznetsky Most. A crowd swarmed around her on the street; and before she could carry the books into the shop, buyers darted inside and emerged with cashier's chits that they pressed on her.

Almost all titles except the dull political tracts that roll off the press endlessly sell rapidly. The classics are constantly in demand. One scrap paper collection campaign proved a huge success in Moscow because, in exchange for old paper, it offered popular books such as Dumas novels and the Ilf and Petrov humorous classics. The Muscovite roams the second-hand bookshops in search of hard-to-get titles, and there is a lively black market in books of every kind.

Moscow has a black market in all sorts of other goods. The typical operator is the sales clerk who tucks a desired item under the counter for a friend and accepts a favour in return; a person selling a used car who goes through the motions of accepting a state appraiser's low estimate for a vehicle and then, with the buyer's connivance, adds several thousand roubles to the price; the workman who smuggles a roll of wire out of the factory and exchanges it for a bottle of vodka; the individual who illegally cuts down a fir tree on the outskirts of town and sells it at the New Year; the profiteer who brings early vegetables to the Moscow markets from the South and sells them for a fancy price. There are also professional speculators who buy up scarce items and sell them at high prices, but they run the risk of penalties ranging from exile as "parasites" to execution for large-scale operations.

The Russian term for these covert activities is "on the left", a sphere of illegal practices that extends to Moscow's taxi service. The city has a fairly efficient and inexpensive cab service, with a ratio of perhaps one cab to each 500 persons. If you order a taxi by phone several hours in advance, you can generally count on it arriving, but hailing one during the rush-hour or late at night can be a frustrating experience, as the already cited incident at the Hotel Rossia indicates. When the Muscovite cannot find a cab or when taxi after taxi with a small green light on its windscreen (signifying that it is supposed to be on duty) speeds past ignoring him, he stands at the kerb and holds up a hand in the hope that any driver "on the left" will take him. If he holds up two fingers, he is indicating that he is willing to pay double the usual fare. The gypsy cab may be a private car or

Drawn to a shop featuring women's wear, citizens cluster in front of the window. The production of consumer goods is erratic and the sought-after items on display may or may not be available inside the shop. The appearance of a high-quality garment in another store (below) soon attracts an eager crowd.

some official's vehicle that the chauffeur is using for private gain. So common are the gypsy cabs that the police pay little attention to them.

As in a legitimate cab or chauffeured car, one of the passengers in a gypsy cab usually sits with the driver, making conversation easier. The man or woman at the wheel can turn out to be a friendly soul. Once, when my wife and I were rushing to catch a train late at night, the driver of a gypsy cab threw himself into the spirit of the chase. He took us to our apartment, waited while we packed our bags, drove us to the station at breakneck speed, arriving two minutes before the train left, and refused payment. "Hurry up," he said, "Never mind the money. You'll risk missing your train. Good luck!"

Years ago, many cab drivers used to refuse tips, but a survey conducted in the 1970s by the *Izvestia* Sunday supplement showed that four out of five Moscow passengers tipped and the gratuities were accepted. In recent years I have met with only one refusal—from a beefy, middle-aged woman driver, with a hoarse voice and a wonderful, deep laugh, who said her childhood dream had been to become a great actress. The next best thing, she said, was to drive a cab and meet interesting people. "Men take offence when I refuse a tip," she told me. "They try to force it on me or leave the money on the seat. I'd rather have a good conversation." We had good conversation.

One organization that must be particularly frustrated by the activities of people "on the left" is the Dawn Service Trust of Moscow, an official body that sends agents from door to door to take orders for apartment improvements and then arranges for them to be made. They ask: Do you want the door insulated with leatherette-covered padding, for extra warmth and quiet? A peephole inserted in the door? Wallpaper hung? Floors refinished? Shelves built? The answer is often no, because "Vasya & Co." got there before the official service trust and had already done the work. There is no real Vasya, of course. "Vasya & Co.", or simply "Uncle Vasya", is a euphemism for workmen operating "on the left". Some are state-employed workers moonlighting in their free time. Others are bold free-booters working at such illegal jobs full time. One Moscow newspaper calculated that of the 14.5 million roubles Muscovites spend each year on household handiwork of the kind I have mentioned, the state service trusts get less than one-third of the business. "Vasya" gets the lion's share.

After the newspaper denounced this state of affairs an anonymous "Uncle Vasya" responded. He sent a letter, saying that not only did he approach the customer first, he and his helpers did the work better than the Dawn Service Trust. The official organization charged low prices, he conceded; but after its agent had taken the householder's order, the state workmen might not turn up for a week or more, and then might do a shoddy job. By contrast, the illicit handymen went to work immediately, cleaned up and left, having made a few quick roubles. They could not afford to dawdle. Working for themselves, without overheads, they earned more than three times what they would be paid for the job by the state, but they also gave full value, he said. "We don't have to get a thousand papers signed before we can hammer in one nail above quota," taunted "Vasya".

Confronted with his letter, the paper retreated from its righteous position. Grudgingly, it conceded the skill of craftsmen who outdid the state service trust; and it proposed sanctioning "Vasya & Co." provided they did not steal their tools and materials from the state. It predicted, however, that the "Vasyas" would end up working for the state service trusts, as had so many other craftsmen. To induce them to accept government jobs, it suggested that they be allowed to moonlight on evenings and weekends. Nothing was done about these proposals. "Vasya & Co." remains illegal—and continues to flourish. Indirectly, the activities of illicit handymen blocked a proposal by the same newspaper to introduce the use of cheque books and credit cards. Almost every Moscow family has a savings account in a state bank, at 2 per cent interest; but payments by cheque are almost unknown. A few factories deposit employees' salaries directly to their savings accounts instead of handing them cash, thus eliminating long queues at the bookkeepers' desks on the twice-monthly pay-days and also removing the temptation for workers to go straight from the bookkeeper to the liquor shop. Newspaper readers suggested that the state go a step further and pay all employees by transfers to banks or credit card accounts. The employees could then pay for state goods by cheque or credit card. One Old Bolshevik even submitted his drawing of a model cheque to show what it would look like. There was a heated debate about the novel idea, and hundreds of letters poured into the newspaper.

But economists quickly squashed the idea. How, they asked, could the state allow cheques or credit cards if they might be used to pay illicit handymen patronized by Muscovites? The proposal foundered on this dilemma. Muscovites continue to live by cash alone.

A Distaff Corps of Labourers

Four female building workers exemplify the "immense, wide-faced, ruddy peasant women" described by playwright Arthur Miller after a visit to Moscow.

Newcomers to Moscow are often taken aback by the frequent sight of hefty women—made positively massive in winter by padded coats, thick gloves and felt boots—at work digging, clearing, lifting and building. To Muscovites, however, female labourers have been an unremarkable feature of city life for decades—and never more so than after the Second World War, when women filled jobs left vacant by men killed in battle. Even today, there is no lack of peasant women willing to undertake the most arduous tasks in order to obtain coveted Moscow residence permits. It is a matter of considerable official pride that on such jobs, workers of both sexes compete on equal terms. Nonetheless, Soviet women are still expected to combine even a strenuous job with their traditional roles of running a household and raising the children.

Wearing the headscarves that are part of the unofficial uniform of Moscow's female labourers, a group of leaf-sweepers gossip before returning to work.

Armed with broad-bladed scrapers and heavily insulated against the biting cold, four street cleaners clear the last shards of ice from a city thoroughfare.

A stooping, grandmotherly figure sweeps up scraps of rubbish in front of the Spassky Tower, the main official gateway to the Kremlin. Two uniformed guards look on disinterestedly from beneath red traffic lights that forbid entrance to all but authorized vehicles.

Bending intently to her task, a handywoman adds a fresh coat of paint to a Moscow railing.

Women construction workers take a break, while below them young Muscovites—whose easier way of life is resented by some older folk—relax in the grass.

With an expression that would do justice to any Detroit hardhat or London docker, a woman construction worker grimaces over her shoulder as she reverses her steamroller to complete repairs on a Moscow street.

6

The Lighter Side of Moscow

When Moscow is not at work, it is a family town. Most leisure is spent in the home, and may involve three generations at once, since frequently parents, children and grandparents live together. There is little night life. Theatres, restaurants and entertainment programmes at the trade union clubs shut down at 10.30. Cinemas and the very few bars and cafés close at 11.00. By midnight streets are deserted even in the centre of town, the Metro is stopping for the night, and the last buses are on their way to the depots through dark and quiet streets. Moscow's way of life is basically that of the early-to-bed, early-to-rise working man. There are sophisticated Muscovites, but Moscow is not sophisticated. It is resolutely proletarian.

It is also a city of women. I would hardly call Moscow a "feminine city"—that is not the phrase for it—but it has been predominantly a city of women since 1914. At the end of the Second World War, which cost the country 20 million lives, Moscow men were outnumbered two to one. By 1970 there were still 852,000 more females than males in a population of more than 7,000,000, but by that time the disproportion was confined to the older generation, and sociologists were reassuring women that there was a man for every marriageable woman.

I recall attending, in 1974, a lecture for young people at which the speaker (a woman) urged brides to demand that their spouses share the household chores because "you no longer need fear that nowadays you will lack for a husband". That remark gives some idea of the pampered state of the Moscow male, and of the burdens that Moscow's working women have had to bear single-handed.

Everyone is familiar with the image of the hefty Russian woman shovelling snow or performing manual labour; it comes as no surprise that Moscow women work, often at hard jobs, and thus carry a double load of job and home cares. What surprised me in recent years was how many strove to be feminine. Women on factory assembly lines wore beehive hairdos (grotesquely capped by big white bandanas while they worked); laughing girl apprentices at a tool plant were clearly influenced by the graceful style of Olga Korbut, the lissome Olympic gymnast; and I was startled when a young woman welder removed her clumsy work gloves to inspect newly manicured fingernails. Plainly, such women were not going to be Mother Heroines of the Soviet Union or earn the Order of Maternal Glory, under the 1944 wartime decree that honoured mothers of seven to ten children or more. Like most Moscow women today, they had (or would have) only one child, or at most two children—in spite of maternal

Silhouetted against a summer moon, the Ostankino Television Tower in Moscow's northern outskirts looks like a futuristic minaret. The 1,700-foot structure, the tallest in the world, can provide Muscovites with an evening out in its revolving restaurant, or an evening at home watching one of the four TV channels beamed from its transmitter.

benefits that include paid maternity leave of nearly four months and subsidized nurseries and kindergartens.

The pressure of job, career and housing shortage kept many from having larger families, but now they also want to "have fun"—a term used by a young woman sexologist with whom I talked—before settling down to motherhood. The fact that she was a sexologist is itself significant. Sexology is a science new to Moscow. By the mid-1970s three long-delayed books on problems of sexual maladjustment had appeared and the first Moscow clinic to treat sex problems had opened. In 1976, for the first time since the 1920s, a Moscow newspaper made a favourable reference to the view expressed by an early Bolshevik feminist, Alexandra Kollontai, that sensual pleasure in sex is important. Puritanism remains strong, but the younger generation is beginning to adopt new urban values.

Although Soviet values are changing and the birthrate is going down, the arrival of a baby is an event to celebrate. One of the more unusual sights of Moscow is the evening appearance of young husbands on the street outside maternity homes. After giving birth, the mother spends about a week in the maternity home. Although the father may view his child through a glass screen, he may not enter the maternity ward, so after work he stands outside the building, smiling and waving or calling to the mother as she stands at the second- or third-storey window. I have sometimes seen mothers toss notes to their husbands waiting on the pavement below.

The tradition that children are treasured possessions remains strong. Parents indulge them; grandparents spoil them. Rarely are youngsters called upon to share family chores. They are waited on, dressed up, and given the best the family has. If there is a delicacy on the table in limited quantity, the children get it. Discipline begins at the age of eight, and soon enough—as they become teenagers—they are expected to give up their bus seats to adults, conform to prim standards of behaviour, and begin the grind of intense competition for admission to schools of higher education. Meanwhile, they luxuriate in the permissiveness of childhood.

Before they reach school age, many of Moscow's children are looked after at day-care centres at modest cost to the parents. As in the West, child-sized furniture, flowers and toys generally provide a cheery setting. Sometimes there are murals of Russian fairytale scenes. The nurseries, which serve about 40 per cent of the city's children between the ages of four months and four years, and the kindergartens, which care for about 70 per cent of youngsters between the ages of four and seven—percentages much higher than in most other Soviet cities—make it possible for Moscow's mothers to combine a career with a family.

The city also provides children with theatres, circuses, puppet shows and Young Pioneer palaces (centres for hobbies and arts). Local neighbourhoods are equipped with numerous small playgrounds, a few of which

Under a coppery western sky, evening traffic moves along Kalinin Prospekt, known as Moscow's "golden mile". The description derives from the modern buildings—offices, shops and apartment buildings—that line the thoroughfare. A showpiece of the 1960s, the broad avenue links the city centre with the Moscow River, where the "Stalin-Gothic" spires of the Ukraine Hotel close the vista.

are laid out with log-cabin play houses and large tree stumps carved into life-size figures of bears, other animals, fairytale characters and medieval knights in armour. Moscow television puts on children's programmes that are better than the often tedious propagandist programmes for adults.

Another honoured category of Muscovites is the aged—the *babushkas* (grandmothers) and *dedushkas* (grandfathers). Persons of retirement age constitute about 20 per cent of the population. Working women may retire at 55, men at 60, but pensions are small, and many of the elderly go on working part-time. There are few institutions for the elderly and almost no retirement communities. With the gradual improvement in rural conditions, Muscovites tell me, some old folk now go back to the villages where they were born, there to enjoy old age (with garden). But even the aged do not lightly surrender residence in Moscow. More often than not, the elderly live with their grown-up children in town (or, more usually, the younger couple will move in with one set of parents).

The tradition of the three-generation household is tenacious. *Babushka* has always been an honoured figure in the Russian family. She is regarded as the matriarch of the clan, ruling with a mixture of asperity and tenderness. Even in crowded conditions, the working mother is glad to have grandma's (and grandpa's) help in running the household. *Babushka* cares for the grandchildren after school hours, and also hands on folklore, recipes, traditions, superstitions, history—and often religion as well. *Dedushka* stands in line for the groceries.

Under an unconventional "big top"—a huge theatre built in 1971 in the shape of a circus tent—members of the Moscow State Circus perform with all the precision and panache that has made them world famous. At left, spotlights catch the controlled elegance of a high-flying gymnast. Above, acrobatic Cossack horsemen thunder round the ring with a banner that proudly names their homeland in the Kuban River area of South Russia.

Babushkas come in two basic models. There is the redoubtable one in black blouse and skirt, probably with several layers of petticoats; and there is the frail and gentle one, with twinkling eyes.

If you want to watch and hear *babushkas* in action, sit near the front of a Moscow bus or tram. Along with invalids and parents carrying small children, the elderly are permitted to enter by the front door, normally an exit; this privilege spares buffeting by the crowds at the rear entrance door. The seats up front are reserved for these categories of passengers, and here the elderly dispense wisdom, gossip and strictures. On a bus, I heard a *babushka*—the kind who will remind a total stranger to pull up his coat collar against the cold—launch into a tirade against two young women seated sideways in order to converse across the aisle. She could not bring herself to express her real complaint, which obviously was that their postures revealed patches of thigh. Instead, in a loud, critical discourse on postures, she told them to face forward. The young women retorted that she herself, in her eagerness to reprove them, had also turned sideways. The passengers burst into laughter and the discomfited *babushka* retreated into muttered grumblings about the disrespectful young.

Seemingly censorious *babushkas* can turn out to have a sense of humour, however. I was walking down a boulevard in summertime when I heard a Beatles tune. Several teenage girls on a bench were huddled around a transistor tape recorder. A *babushka* approached from the other direction; she was heavy-set and potato-faced and I expected her to upbraid the girls for playing the tape recorder outdoors. The *babushka* advanced firmly until she came abreast of the girls. Then suddenly her face cracked into a grin and she broke into a peasant dance step, holding one hand aloft as if it were waving a handkerchief, and swinging her ample black skirt with the other. As soon as she passed the girls, she resumed her firm tread with no further sign of emotion. The girls gaped.

You'll run into *babushkas* and *dedushkas* at the markets, where they are likely to offer advice on the quality of the foods. One old man gave my wife and me an instructive lecture on how to pick the sweetest melons and which parts of the country raised the best—all this interlarded with reminiscences of his village on the Volga and the story of his wife's illness. "Ever since the war," he said, "I haven't been quite right in my mind. I weep easily, and people think it strange; but I love people, and I find them at the market, so I come here to meet them."

You will also see the elderly working as guards or attendants at theatres and museums. At the doors of galleries they sit on straight-backed chairs, seemingly fierce guardians, viewing you as intruders—until you speak with them. To conserve electricity, some museums keep the lighting dim until visitors fill the rooms, but the attendants will be glad to turn on additional lights for you if you ask.

They respond to a show of interest. Some can give livelier lectures than

Red Schoolhouses

When Moscow children start school at the age of seven, they enter a world of stern convention and disciplined effort, where ideology and obedience are as important as neat writing and multiplication tables. All the children wear uniform, usually black dresses for the girls and navy blue jackets and trousers for the boys. Soviet teaching methods rely heavily on rote learning and moral exhortation. Seven-year-olds, for instance, receive a star-shaped badge with an inset showing Lenin as a child, and earn the right to keep it by good behaviour. But as these pictures of School No. 479 indicate, each pupil's individuality shows through the superficial uniformity and air of solemnity.

Attentive seven-year-olds work in the classroom.

Strict but warm, the teacher allows herself a smile.

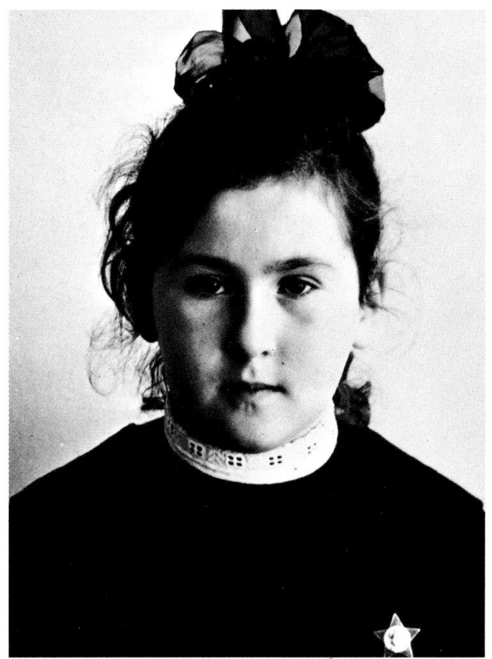

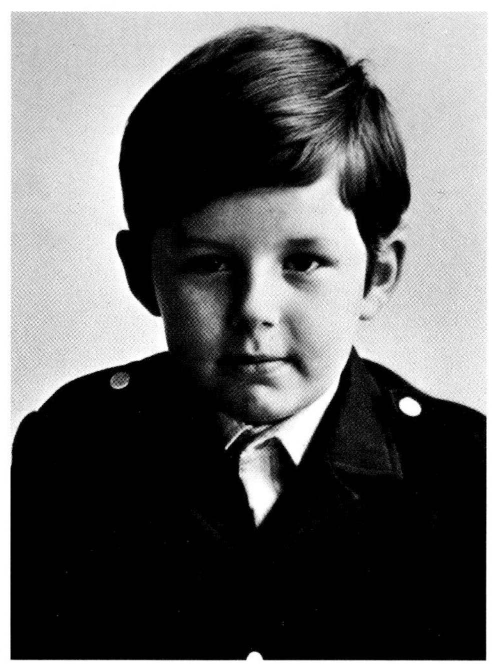

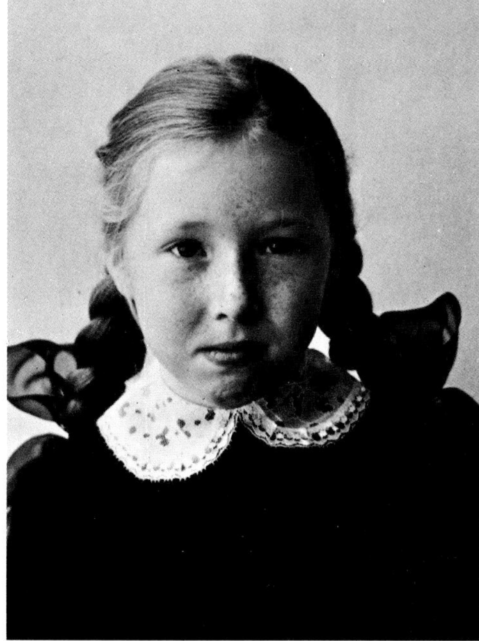

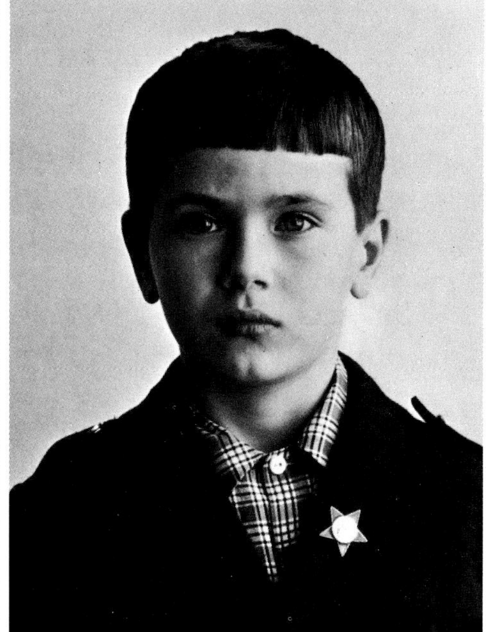

Red stars and Pioneer scarves add a touch of colour to the children's otherwise sombre uniforms, while ambitious hair-ribbons give distinction to the girls.

the guides. One day at the Pushkin Art Museum my wife paused before a model of the Parthenon, and a sturdy *babushka* standing beside her launched upon histories of the Greek gods and goddesses that were depicted on the pediment, discussing them as if they were neighbours, personal friends or members of her family. She didn't know many of the names, she confessed; but this one, she said pointing, stole that one's wife, and the goddess over there fell in love with the god on her right; the character at that side used to deliver messages, like a postman, and this one here was always fighting.

Yet another place where you are likely to see old people is the cloakroom of all public buildings—a Russian institution and a necessary one in winter when people wear heavy outerwear. Heaven forbid that you take your coat to your theatre seat; it is considered uncultured. Theatre cloakrooms, in combination with the large lobbies where the audiences first queue to surrender and later to reclaim hats, coats, scarves and overshoes, seem to take up as much space as the auditoriums themselves. The elderly attendants bustle back and forth along the rows of hangers, with huge heaps of heavy overcoats in their arms. (Cinemas are an exception. With one audience arriving just as another is leaving, and with showings about every two hours, cloakrooms would be madhouses. Movie theatres alone, therefore, dispense with the service—and always keep the premises chilly enough to permit street clothing to be worn comfortably indoors.)

Moscow offers a wide choice of theatrical entertainment. There are more than 30 theatres with a total of 40,000 seats, and on any given evening they present more than 20 plays, two operas, an operetta or two, a gypsy performance, two puppet shows for adults (the children have their turn at matinees), two or three plays for young people, a music hall programme, and a mimed play for the deaf. I do not count the two single-ring circuses, which are high theatre in themselves. All the theatre and circus seats are filled nightly, and tickets are difficult to get.

Sir Bernard Pares, a British historian, summed up the Moscow theatre in his remark, "Russians love a pageant". The abundance of lavish productions, the drama and the colour—in short, the pageantry—overwhelm the first-time visitor. On each return to Moscow, I revel initially in the riches of the Moscow theatre. But soon enough I find a sameness about it. I tire of the traditional, realistic style of almost all the productions. I become irritably conscious of propaganda overtones even in presentations of the classics. I yearn for a touch of verve, originality of theme, and maybe just a bit of silliness. Sergei Obrastsov's sophisticated puppet shows at the theatre which bears his name meet those requirements; if only the repertoire were wider and a puppet theatre could be large enough to meet the demand for tickets! The Taganka and the Sovremennik (Contemporary) theatres, two fringe or "off-Broadway" companies, strive valiantly to be innovative. In 1973, when the Contemporary Theatre started to produce plays "in the round", it came as a novelty—this in Moscow, the city where the great director Vsevolod Meyerhold was one of the world's most renowned theatrical innovators, until he was purged in 1938.

Propaganda and censorship, bad as they are, are not the only considerations that mar Moscow's theatre. There is also the staleness that comes of a system of entrenched permanent repertory companies. Since each of the 25 companies has at least six plays in its repertoire, and most have more, there is theoretically a choice of well over a hundred productions to be seen each season, not to mention those of out-of-town companies visiting on tour. But a number of theatres stage the same plays more or less simultaneously, and most of the theatres keep the same approved productions on the boards season after season. I have seen some productions that had been kept going more than 30 years—in a few cases with one or two of the same actors or actresses.

Perhaps it is churlish for a foreigner to cavil when offered the abundance of the Moscow stage. But I think many Muscovites might agree with me. Most would not give up the classical perfectionism of the Bolshoi Ballet, product of a 200-year tradition and of the rigorous nine-year training of dancers in the Bolshoi's studio-school. But when a rare experimental dance group, such as the Yakobson Leningrad Choreographic Miniatures, comes to town, the cheers of the audience indicate how refreshing they find the performances. Muscovites would not do without the Moscow Art Theatre—although some compare it to a relic preserved under a glass bell—but they have taken it for granted for many decades; it is the new productions at the Taganka and the Contemporary theatres that arouse their real excitement.

Because of the 7.00 p.m. curtain time, anyone who wants to savour Moscow's evenings must choose between the theatre and dining out. Few restaurants start to serve before 7.00; and even there, because service is slow, it is hopeless to expect dinner by curtain time, and when one emerges from the theatre, the restaurants will be closed or closing.

Muscovites regard restaurants somewhat as a Westerner regards a night club or discotheque. They come to spend the entire evening—dancing, mingling, drinking and, almost incidentally, dining. Although only two Moscow restaurants present a floor show, most do have orchestras and dance floors. Unless you warn the waiter that you wish to be served quickly, and perhaps remind him at each course to serve the next without delay, he will assume that you are there for entertainment and conversation and are in no hurry. The waiter provides only one menu to a table (you may have to ask for it; he guards it jealously). Probably printed years ago, the menu will include every dish the restaurant has ever served or hoped to serve. It lists the chef's total repertoire, so to speak, not merely the dishes available on the given evening.

Except in a few staid restaurants, mostly in foreigners' hotels, the atmosphere tends to be informal and convivial. If a table is not fully occupied, it is considered normal for strangers to take the empty seats. A group at another table may send over a bottle for you to drink their health —a way of getting acquainted. Men invite women to dance without the formality of introductions. A woman, too, may ask a stranger from another table to dance with her. Celebrating parties sometimes break into song or start up a folk dance in a corner even while others are gliding around the floor to ballroom music. The waiter leaves it to the host or toastmaster at each table to pour the drinks for his party.

Except in a few restaurants which feature the Near Eastern cuisine of the Transcaucasus or the cooking of Soviet Central Asia, the food is Russian —even in restaurants with names like Berlin, Budapest, Havana, Peking, Prague, Sofia and Warsaw. I love the array of hors d'oeuvres, soups (the test of a true Russian soup is whether a fork, plunged into it, will stand up unsupported), fish, mushrooms, dairy products, breads, pancakes and *kasha* (buckwheat groats). But I find the meat dishes generally uninspired, and the selection of vegetables limited. Caviar, once plentiful, has been a

Although Moscow's restaurants have a reputation for slow service and predictable food, some are impressively decorated and furnished. The Slavic Bazaar (below), preserves the old charm that made it popular with artists in the early 1900s. In the Hotel Ukraine (below right) a huge chandelier offers a touch of grandeur to diners watching a floorshow.

rarity in Moscow since the 1960s because of past over-fishing, poaching, and construction of dams on the Volga and also because much of it is exported. Most of Moscow's caviar is now reserved for foreign-currency tourists, and the price is high.

I think exotic food from the forests may some day replace caviar and sturgeon as Moscow delicacies. A chain of five Moscow shops, poetically called "Gifts of Nature" or "Bounty of the Russian Forests", has been opened by rural co-operatives to sell game, berries of varieties little known in the West, many kinds of honey, and jars of soup prepared from peasant recipes. At one of these shops on Komsomolsky Prospekt my wife and I found venison of Siberian deer, Manchurian deer, elk and musk deer; wild boar, hazel grouse, wood grouse, willow grouse, ptarmigan, heathcock and partridge; quail eggs, ransom (a wide-leafed wild garlic used in salads and for seasoning), rowanberries, red whortleberry jam and the Russian cranberry called *klyukva.* Two Moscow restaurants specialize in game, including bear and elk steaks.

What restaurants lack in variety of food, they make up for in noise—especially those restaurants with bands. Many of the tunes are Western

and many of the songs are sung in English. I have met some Soviet performers whose English was excellent, but also a few who did not know the language in which they were singing. They memorized the sounds of words they did not understand.

Rock was still frowned upon in the mid-1970s, but it was winning gradual —if tardy—acceptance, being performed by scores of amateur ensembles in Moscow and by hundreds of them throughout the country. Some of these amateur groups were very good, but authorities were reluctant to allow them to give public performances. When rock was played, it was mostly for small, exclusive gatherings. The most successful social event arranged by the United States Embassy for the foreign colony in 1975 was a rock concert by a youthful Soviet ensemble that presented an abridgement of *Jesus Christ Superstar* in English. And one of the most successful series of lecture-concerts at the central Moscow lecture hall in 1974 was a review of the history of Soviet jazz, played by bands from the Baltic, Leningrad, the Caucasus and Moscow.

In the Soviet lexicon "jazz" covers the whole range from blues to rock. A few original, "unofficial" works by young Soviet jazz and rock composers showed genuine talent. One of the composers told me he had trouble with lyrics, however, for a peculiar reason, which partly explained why the restaurant singers sang foreign tunes in English instead of translating the lyrics. Russian, he pointed out, is a polysyllabic language, incompatible with a musical framework built on the terse rhythms of English. "I'll kiss your lips" requires four syllables in English, but the same sentence in Russian takes eight—difficult to squeeze into a bar of hard rock. So, for the most part, Moscow swings in English. Loudly.

The young flock to a half dozen Moscow cafés where jazz and, occasionally, watered-down rock are heard. During the 1960s an effort was made to establish non-alcoholic youth cafés as recreation centres offering music, amateur entertainment, poetry readings and soft drinks. They were too successful. As long as such cafés were few and experimental, the Young Communist League and the trade unions were able to subsidize them, but when their numbers began to grow in the mid-1960s they became too expensive to operate. At least that is how the *Izvestia* Sunday supplement explained their demise. Eventually they were replaced by commercial cafés serving cocktails and meals, and providing commercial entertainment —pale imitations of Western discotheques.

If Muscovites seeking an evening's entertainment find some of the plays turgid, the restaurants noisy and the cafés full, at least they need have little or no fear for their personal safety while strolling home. Moscow by night seems to be one of the safer cities of the world. I venture this statement on the basis of personal observation and the opinion of long-time foreign residents. I cannot support it with statistics, because Soviet crime statistics are not published. Nor can I base a judgement on Press reports, because Moscow papers rarely report violence when it does occur. Such crimes as one reads about are mostly "economic crimes": speculation (profiteering), embezzlement, and the theft of state property.

Rumour feeds on the policy of news suppression. In the autumn of 1974 some Muscovites were warned at their places of work that a Jack the Ripper was loose. Rumours spread. Housewives took to barring their doors. Husbands met their spouses and walked them home from the Metro stations. Gossip magnified the story until some people whispered that whole gangs were operating. At the height of the scare, a deputy police commissioner gave an interview to a Moscow daily, blandly denying that any serious crimes had been committed during the preceding ten days. That same day, foreign correspondents learned, the attacker was apprehended and charged with a dozen assaults upon women, several of which had indeed been committed within the preceding ten days.

Petty crime and, of course, crimes of passion persist. I personally know of several car thefts; and pilfering of hard-to-get car accessories is common. But housebreaking seems rare, and holdups with firearms are almost unheard of; firearms are strictly controlled. Occasionally *babushkas* mutter that they have heard of a purse-snatching or "undressing"—that is, the theft of hat and coat at knife-point in some dark alley.

The village-community atmosphere of Moscow—preserved by so many first- and second-generation Muscovites—seems to me a factor in creating the sense of personal safety. In summer, *babushkas* sit after dark talking together in the courtyards of apartment buildings as if the yards were extensions of their living rooms. A Moscow friendship, and surely courtship, is inconceivable without long walks (particularly in view of the crowded housing). Lovers occupy park benches on the boulevards late at night, even in the snows of winter. Some strollers are about even when the city seems asleep, and any late-night driver is apt to be hailed by stray walkers or partygoers seeking a ride home. If the driver wants to give them a ride, either in the gypsy-cab tradition or simply out of friendliness, he does so without fear.

The only "crimes" a visitor is likely to witness are measured by most Westerners as minor social problems. Prostitution has been almost eliminated. Narcotics addiction is almost unknown. Not so what Russians call "hooliganism", which to them means a whole range of rowdy behaviour committed while under the influence of alcohol—anything from loud speech and wife-beating to knife-fights. Drinking is a longstanding problem in Russia. In the old days an entire village would occasionally indulge in a week-long binge fuelled by home brew and ending in a violent free-for-all on the village green. After the First World War, Russia—like the United States and Finland—tried prohibition briefly. It didn't work and, as in Finland and the U.S., it was abandoned.

The massive columns of the Bolshoi's portico live up to the theatre's name: "Bolshoi" means "big" or "grand". Opened in 1780, the theatre has been destroyed twice by fire, but was rebuilt in 1824 and again in 1856. In addition to being the home of opera and ballet, the sumptuous red-and-gold interior (below) was once the scene of Party meetings and Soviet congresses addressed by Lenin himself.

Since the Second World War, to judge by expressions of concern in the Press and by statistics showing greatly increased vodka consumption, drinking has grown as a social problem. It may not have reverted to the scale of the distant past, but it troubles the authorities and a large part of the Moscow public. In recent years the hours of sale for liquor have been restricted, prices have been increased, laws and campaigns have been introduced to curb excessive drinking, but with little effect.

Russians call intoxication "the green snake", equivalent roughly to our expression about "seeing pink elephants". I cannot imagine a more determined adversary of "the green snake" than the Moscow housewife. She is tolerant of social drinking around the family table, and of human frailty generally. Guests commonly bring a bottle when they are invited to a family dinner or party; such occasions are simply incomplete without an array of bottles on the table. The tradition of the toast reigns, and each toast requires another in response. But male drinking outside the home, especially drinking that leads to brawling, turns the Moscow housewife into a temperance dragon. At a public lecture on current events I heard a woman ask during the question period whether it was true that the Soviet Union was about to import Pepsi-Cola from the United States. Yes, the lecturer replied, in exchange for exports of Soviet vodka. "Let's send them all of our vodka and get rid of it!" the woman cried. The audience, mostly women, burst into cheers and applause.

Drinking among men has an element of *machismo* about it. Almost every foreign male who has resided in Moscow has experienced the ritual challenge to a succession of drinks "bottoms up". Once, when a Moscow companion ordered a vodka at a restaurant and I declined to join him, he insisted on ordering for me anyway; the waiter, he argued, would consider an order for less than 200 grams (about two-thirds of a pint) "an insult". (Was the waiter, I wondered, thinking about his sales quota?)

The serious Moscow drinker may start on Friday evening, pause for a few hours of sobriety on Saturday, resume on Saturday evening, go on late into Sunday night, and often miss work the next day, causing factory managers to complain of "lost Mondays". Drinkers looking for companions to share a bottle stand around liquor shops. If one of them holds two fingers discreetly at the lapel, it is a signal that he is seeking two fellow-drinkers to share a quick bottle. The custom arose when a bottle of vodka cost three roubles. The price has almost doubled, but the expression *na troyikh*, "divide by three", remains part of the language. When the common drinking glass is missing from a street vending machine that dispenses soft drinks (there is a rinsing device on the machine at which each customer washes the glass before use), Muscovites blame vodka drinkers, saying they probably took the glass in order to divide a bottle "by three".

Although vast amounts of public criticism are levelled at the heavy drinker, he has been traditionally treated with compassion. Several times

in the 1930s I encountered drunks sprawled on the pavement. Whenever I met such a scene in winter, there was always some passer-by trying to rouse the drunk so that he would not freeze to death. Failing, the good Samaritan was likely to carry him into the shelter of any near-by doorway. But today you aren't likely to stumble over drunks on the streets of Moscow.

In recent years I have sometimes seen a tipsy Muscovite lurching along, usually helped home by wife or fellow-tipplers, but it is a long time since I have seen any drinker stretched out on the pavement. There is good reason for this. The police or their volunteer aides, the *druzhinniki*, have hauled him off to a sobering-up station, where he is given a shower, hot coffee, a bed, and charged for these services the next morning with what amounts to a fine of 15 roubles. Furthermore, his place of work is likely to be notified; and he may find his photograph on a bulletin board there, along with an account of his misdemeanour. Repeated offences may entail the risk of appearing before a "comrades' court" or a committee of neighbours and shopmates.

There are some half million of these *druzhinniki* in the city, each of whom contributes one evening a month without pay to patrol public places in his own neighbourhood. The most important task of the *druzhinniki* (the word means "detachment members") is to prevent or stop hooliganism. They have no uniforms or weapons, only red armbands, whistles to summon aid if necessary, and red cards authorizing them to demand identification from violators of public order. All serious crimes they leave to the regular police.

Druzhinniki are usually men in their thirties, selected by the Communist Party, the Young Communist League and the trade unions. A very few special patrols whose responsibility is the young are made up of volunteers in their twenties and include women. These youth patrols are assigned to places where the young generation congregates, particularly cafés, dance floors, and the neighbourhoods of technical colleges and universities. (Back in the 1960s *druzhinniki* in a few towns constituted themselves as guardians of public morals until Moscow newspapers denounced their attempts to decree the length of hair or kinds of dress permitted in public places. The *druzhinniki* yielded.)

I went on patrol one evening as a correspondent to find out how young *druzhinniki* operate. A police captain—the deputy chief of Sverdlov Borough Precinct No. 17, in the centre of Moscow—briefed us. He listed the bars, cafés, a cinema and the back alleys we were to inspect on our rounds. We were to keep an eye out for drunks or altercations, and to escort any offenders to *druzhinniki* headquarters, a two-room apartment furnished with a table, chairs, a few benches, wall posters and a telephone. There, I was told, offenders would be warned if their misbehaviour was minor. If the offence were more serious, a record might be made and sent to his Communist Party unit or to the Young Communist League, or to the trade union at the offender's place of work. Or, if matters warranted, the offender might be turned over to the police. We were not to use force. The police captain assured me it would not be necessary, such was the authority of our red armbands.

We stopped at one restaurant where, we had been told, recently some patrons had tippled and become obstreperous. The manager assured us all was well. At an outdoor café there was a squabble between two young men over seating. But before our patrol could reach the table where the seat was being loudly contested, two *druzhinniki* from a different detachment moved in to settle the dispute. At a busy street corner we stopped a young man from crossing against the lights. The alleys were empty. The suspicious-looking loiterer whom we saw outside the cinema turned out to be waiting for a friend. The only thing we contributed to law and order that evening was our presence.

Druzhinniki help to police the crowds on May Day and on November 7, and around churches at Easter and Christmas. On occasions when churches are heavily attended, *druzhinniki* have been fairly efficient about organizing the human traffic and are generally respectful to the religious. Sometimes, however, they have turned away young people, claiming that they came simply out of curiosity (which may well have been true) and might create a disturbance (unlikely). In addition, *druzhinniki* have been employed at the trials of dissidents; the dissidents say that by packing the courtrooms, they have kept out sympathizers of the defendants.

Quiet, orderly and family-oriented, Moscow may be a metropolis, but it is certainly not a cosmopolitan one. The very word "cosmopolitan" was made a term of opprobrium—a brand tantamount to "traitor"—during the purges of the early 1950s, at a time when Soviet propaganda trumpeted that Russians had invented the steam engine, the radio, the aeroplane and the jet engine, and when some Jews were being denounced as "homeless cosmopolitans". The Stalin purges may be past, but the word "cosmopolitan" remains pejorative. "Internationalist", on the other hand, is an approved word, applied in politics and ideology; but it has very little to do with the flavour of everyday life. Muscovites exhibit a tremendous curiosity about the outer world, but their city is as Russian as cabbage soup.

Moscow boasts that its inhabitants include representatives of most of the 110 nationalities of the Soviet Union, and students from more than 135 foreign countries as well. Yet the Moscow population is overwhelmingly, almost 90 per cent Russian. The minorities—Jews, Ukrainians, Tatars, Georgians, Armenians and others—are comparatively few in number and sprinkled among the predominant Russians. The largest minority, the Jews, who number a quarter of a million, play a large part in Moscow's arts and sciences. One sometimes sees Central Asians clustered around the Uzbekistan Restaurant, Jews at the city's single synagogue on high holy days, Africans and Orientals near the higher educational institutions (particularly Patrice Lumumba University); but Moscow has no ethnic enclaves.

If there is a segregated group in Moscow, it is the foreign colony of diplomats, correspondents and businessmen. In any capital, diplomats are likely to be set apart, what with their privileges, their diplomatic licence plates, and their guarded embassies. In many countries, resident foreigners may also be kept under surveillance. Moscow, however, has carried such segregation to the extreme. My wife and I—like other members of the foreign colony—were assigned to an apartment in housing compounds that were watched night and day by a policeman in a sentry box at the entrance. The sentries question and warn off Soviet citizens who lack authorization to mingle with foreigners.

Telephone numbers of foreigners and foreign establishments are excluded from the city phone directory. Large parts of the Soviet Union and some parts of the city itself are off-bounds to foreigners (a restriction to which other countries have reacted in kind), and my wife and I had to obtain permission each time we wished to travel. Traffic police stationed in booths on all main roads leading out of town, and at all major crossroads in the course of an out-of-town journey, stop any cars with the conspicuously different licence plates assigned to foreigners, unless the police at these booths have a record that permission has been granted for the car to travel that route on that day. (Some of the travel restrictions were eased in 1976 after the Helsinki accord.)

Most resident foreigners assume that their telephones are tapped; that their apartment walls contain listening devices, and that their local secretaries, drivers and housemaids report to Soviet officials in detail about their movements, visitors and behaviour. Some Westerners have been openly followed about town. One American correspondent who was being conspicuously followed, apparently in an effort to unnerve him—his despatches had displeased the Soviet authorities—or to warn off Soviet citizens who might speak with him, informed his fellow correspondents. They joined up and proceeded to follow the followers, creating a small procession of cars, like the procession of people stuck to the golden goose in Asbjornsen's fairy tale, "The Princess Who Never Laughed".

Hemmed in as they are, foreign correspondents, businessmen and embassy and consular staffs jest about the "golden ghetto" in which they move; and they amuse one another by repeating stories about foreign visitors in the past—harking back all the way to feudal times—which confirm that outside nationals even then suffered the same suspicion, segregation and surveillance. One American correspondent recounted a story of a Soviet official, talking with a foreigner at an embassy reception, who recalled happily how he had been invited to spend a weekend in a private citizen's home during a visit abroad. "Why doesn't that happen here?" the foreigner asked. The Soviet official quickly changed the subject.

It does happen. In spite of the barriers, a foreign correspondent or businessman may strike up an acquaintance with a Soviet private citizen and be invited to a Moscow home. It happens only after the Muscovite has gained confidence in the foreigner's discretion. There have been so many instances of the police arresting and questioning Soviet citizens who were acquainted with foreigners, so much talk of espionage and the need for "vigilance" towards foreigners, so many cases of foreigners who quoted Soviet citizens in ways that brought down official wrath, that, not surprisingly, most Muscovites are chary of contact with aliens.

Ironically, the one group least deterred by the barriers surrounding the foreigner is the handful of Moscow dissidents, representing every variety of idea from religious dissent against the Soviet system to a brand of Marxism critical of the regime. Some have already served terms in jails or prison camps and feel they have little more to lose and everything to gain by telling their story to the outside world. Their boldness in approaching foreigners, often at great risk to themselves, is in contrast with the timidity of non-political Muscovites; it enlarges their image in the eyes of the correspondents and sometimes endows them with the aura of spokesmen for those many Muscovites whom the foreigner does not meet.

But when the foreigner *is* finally invited into a home, the atmosphere of cold official suspicion is dispelled and he discovers the great warmth and real hospitality of Moscow. The guest is plied with food. "Eat, eat," is the hearty admonition. To abstain is to offend the host. The visitor is overwhelmed with all the friendship of which Muscovites are intrinsically capable. At the kitchen table he meets *babushka* and *dedushka*. The children climb over him with winning affection. Here he finds Moscow the family town: Moscow without parades or politics, the Moscow that, regrettably, few foreigners see intimately, the Moscow of the Muscovites.

A Tradition of Perfection

PHOTOGRAPHS BY PETE TURNER

Some Bolshoi dancers limber up and others wait in attitudes of unconscious grace to begin the practice class that is an essential part of their daily routine.

After 200 years, Moscow's Bolshoi Ballet retains its mystique and drawing power—in spite of increasing criticism that it is "the best 19th-Century ballet of the 20th Century". The production of "Ivan the Terrible", photographed here during rehearsals and at a performance, is a recent addition to the company's broad repertoire; but its florid, dramatic style and theme are firmly in the Russian tradition. Choreographic innovations are confined mainly to stage effects. The company can afford to ignore charges that it is conservative: for purity of technique and passionate sincerity of interpretation the Bolshoi is without equal. These qualities are cultivated assiduously at daily practice classes that are taught by geniuses of the previous generation and attended democratically by even the greatest of the company's dancers.

A revered instructor teaches the poise that once made her a Bolshoi star.

The company's prima ballerina works on her technique with concentration.

Led by the prima ballerina (foreground), the class sinks smoothly into a deep plié, their calm faces as perfectly controlled as their highly trained muscles.

Even in the bare setting of a practice studio, a male soloist vividly projects the emotion of the part he is rehearsing with the prima ballerina.

On the darkened stage a spotlight picks out a knot of dancers rehearsing "Ivan the Terrible", choreographed in 1975 to music by Prokofiev.

The soloist dancing the role of Ivan rehearses the moment when he must hang tautly on bell ropes and swing across stage, towards the audience.

At night, costumes, lighting and the indefinable magic of the performance transform the dancers from hard-working athletes into dramatic, fleeting shapes.

In the performance of "Ivan", the Bolshoi corps shows the impeccable timing and effortless grace born of years devoted to rigorously disciplined training.

Before a sumptuous curtain bearing the U.S.S.R.'s symbol, the soloists accept the audience's applause. None of the 2,155 tickets for each show goes unsold.

7

Facing the Future

From a huge red May Day banner stretched before GUM's frontage, idealized portraits of Lenin, Engels and Marx (left to right) gaze out resolutely—eyes seemingly fixed on the future. Lenin continues to be invoked in all aspects of Soviet life, as much in the role of fatherly guardian as that of political theorist.

The officials who govern Moscow possess powers that city administrators elsewhere would envy. With this sweeping authority, and with a still unfinished city to be moulded, they have a unique opportunity—in theory, at least—to create a model community. Are they likely to succeed? Who are these officials, and how do they obtain their mandate? How do they exercise their powers? What kind of city are they trying to build?

Just think about what Moscow's city managers can do. Only the state can own land, and in Moscow only the city authorities can allocate it. They can withhold it from a prospective user—even, in theory, from such an influential one as a government ministry or leading industry. They assign land without charge and take it without payment (thus, since land carries no cost, the generous use of space around new buildings). They determine the location, size and design of all shops and dwellings. The city owns 90 per cent of the housing—excepting only the co-operatives and the few remaining private homes—and its officials assign the flats.

Together with the Supreme Soviet of the Russian Republic, whose capital Moscow is, they can even control the size of the city. During a single day in August, 1960, they increased its census by almost one million and its area two and a half times by extending Moscow's boundaries. At the same time, they set limits on growth—limits they enforce by deciding who may or may not come here to live, and by stipulating which industries may or may not operate in the city. In 1975, for example, they expelled 95 large factories to reduce the concentration of industry in Moscow. They impose fines not merely on enterprises that pollute the air or water, but also on the personal earnings of the directors of such enterprises—where a fine hurts most.

To finance their programmes, Moscow's governing officials have at their disposal all the funds the city can use. In 1975 the Russian Republic government contributed only 33 per cent of the city's budget, but Moscow itself neither levies taxes nor borrows funds to make up the remainder. It provides all the usual municipal services and many more besides, conducts a massive programme of building and expansion, but even so ends each year with a budget surplus. It seems that this communist municipality is profit-making.

The fact is that Moscow is much more than a municipality in the Western sense; it is also one of the world's largest business conglomerates, owning, operating—and reaping profits from—almost all the cafés, restaurants, hotels (except those run by Intourist for foreign tourists), the taxi companies, the theatres, bakeries, retail trades, local consumer-goods manufacturing, the service trades such as dry cleaning and hair dressing, and a construction industry that sells entire prefabricated apartment buildings to other cities as well as to Moscow itself. Part of the profits from these businesses helps pay for municipal services and development. Even the Metro, which charges only five kopeks a ride, regardless of distance, yields a profit, which subsidises the unprofitable surface transport.

The power wielded by the capital's municipal officials, and the funds and facilities at their disposal are unique even by Soviet standards. Most of the country's other cities depend for funds largely on big industries and grants from the budgets of higher provincial Soviets. From the viewpoint of their mayors or, for that matter, the mayors of Western municipalities, the financial freedom and powers enjoyed by Moscow's city managers might seem Utopian. In reality, however, the city's governing officials have problems of their own. The sheer scale of the administrative structure causes headaches; altogether, the municipality employs 1,400,000 persons—about one of every three adults. To oversee this workforce, and to control the city's business interests and run a big city besides, the officials must possess technical and economic skills as well as managerial qualifications. And, of course, they must also be expert politicians. They answer not only to the Muscovites, but to the central Soviet government, the Communist Party and authorities of the Russian Republic; for Moscow is a double capital: that of the country as a whole and of the republic, the country's largest territorial unit, which has immediate jurisdiction over the city. They must co-ordinate their work with a bureaucratic maze of numerous outside ministries, departments and agencies that are involved as city suppliers or consumers, and they must balance local needs against powerful nationwide interests and pressures.

What sort of person is qualified to handle all of these roles? First of all, any high-ranking member of the city administration is likely to be a favoured member of the Party, for in all Soviet institutions the managers and Party officialdom are intertwined. In Moscow, as elsewhere, higher Party bodies appoint, nominate or approve the local Party leaders and local administrators, and set the policies. The local administrators, headed by the mayor and his aides, then carry out the policies under local Party supervision. Party officials and administrators undergo the same schooling: Party training in addition to technical and administrative education. The local Party executives become involved in the administrative problems, and the administrators help set policy.

The titular head of the city's administration is "the Moscow Soviet" (council), a body of 1,160 deputies, most of them unsalaried, who are nominated or approved by the Party organisation. Nomination is tantamount to election, since there is only one party on the ballot; and the approximately 1,000,000 Party members in Moscow (about twice the nationwide

New Moscow apartment houses, uniform in all their details, interior and exterior, form clusters that ring Moscow. The city still suffers from a chronic housing shortage, in spite of a boom in such construction.

average in proportion to population) get out the vote. It is an honour to be a deputy, but the individual deputy has little direct influence on the day to day governing of the city. The deputies serve on various commissions that help shape the city's administration policies. They also act as intermediaries between the public and city officials; they receive appeals, complaints and petitions from their constituents, intercede for them with the municipal authorities and serve on committees that advise the executive bodies or monitor the work of city agencies. The Soviet meets only four times a year, however. Effective governance rests with an Executive Committee of 25 members, including two Party representatives.

The key figures are the mayor, whose proper title is Chairman of the Executive Committee, and the Moscow Party chief, formally known as the City First Secretary. Indicating how Party and administration interlock, the mayor and the secretary sit on each other's boards, and both positions carry simultaneous membership in the nationwide councils of Party and government alike: the powerful 250-member Communist Party Central Committee and the country's nominal legislature, the Supreme Soviet.

Moscow's municipal executives rank high in both hierarchies. In the Party, the city's secretariat has been a stepping stone to a seat on the 15-member *Politburo*, the pinnacle of Kremlin power. One who stepped from First Secretary of Moscow to *Politburo* member, and eventually

to First Secretary of the Communist Party of the whole country, was Nikita Khrushchev. In the government, the office of mayor of Moscow also has led to top positions at the nationwide level. Nikolai Bulganin, for instance, rose from mayor to Premier.

The backgrounds of the persons who run the city therefore tell something about the makeup of the Soviet leadership as a whole. I have traced the careers of six Moscow secretaries from Stalin's time to 1975 and of the four mayors during this period. Some I met at interviews, Press conferences or diplomatic receptions. All were of Russian nationality and almost all were born in villages or small towns; only one, to the best of my knowledge, was a native of the capital. All, including the mayors, were Party members who were chosen for the upper *nomenklatura* (the list of leading positions) and subsequently were sent to the special schools that the Party maintains to prepare such persons for high office. All, including the secretaries, held technical or engineering diplomas—even Yekaterina Furtseva, the only woman among them; she graduated from a chemical technology institute as well as from a civil aviation academy, became Moscow's Party Secretary, then a member of the *Politburo*, and Minister of Culture from 1960 to 1974.

The executives whom I met at various times impressed me as persons who would have made their mark in any city in the world, none more so than Mayor Vladimir F. Promyslov, whom I interviewed in 1975. Promyslov had a prominent career in the Party, the government of the Russian Republic and the construction industry before becoming mayor in 1963. At one time he had been Deputy Minister of Higher Education for the entire U.S.S.R. But most of his life, as he put it, he has been "building things". He was a civil engineer by training and moved into the mayor's office from that of Minister of Construction of the Russian Republic. His Chaika limousine could often be seen parked at Moscow's new housing construction projects while he inspected them with a practised eye. The long-range plans for the new Moscow were launched during his lengthy term in office, and he played a critical role in their drafting and adoption.

Distinguished, and with features that seemed youthful for a man in his sixties, Mayor Promyslov projected an air of vigour and common sense. He received me, together with another American correspondent, in the city hall on Soviet Square.

The city hall is one of those structures that has had two storeys added to it, and was moved back 45 feet during the widening of Gorky Street during Stalin's time. It has been modernized to meet the needs of the growing city administration, but retains the marks of Czarist splendour. It was built in 1872, to serve in pre-revolutionary times as the residence of the city's governor-general. On the square before it stands a statue, erected a quarter of a century ago to celebrate the city's 800th anniversary; it

Cranes stand motionless against the setting sun. By day they are busy in a drive to meet the planners' target of an apartment for every Moscow family by 1985.

represents the legendary founder of Moscow: Yuri Dolgoruky, son of an illustrious prince of Kiev.

To reach the mayor's conference room we ascended a great marble staircase to a trophy room. Massive wooden doors opened on to a conference room furnished like the ones in almost every Soviet establishment. I have been in scores of them, and each had a long table with about a dozen chairs on each side, a large desk for the chairman of the meeting at the end of the table, and the inevitable portrait of Lenin. This room, however, was larger and more imposing than almost any I could recall, including the relatively modest room in the Kremlin where General Secretary Brezhnev presided at the *Politburo's* Thursday afternoon sessions.

The mayor sat down at the table. In a two-hour interview he described the problems of managing the city administration and outlined Moscow's construction plans for the final quarter of the 20th Century.

Ambitious as the plans were, the most striking thing about them, to one like myself who had witnessed the Moscow boom, was not their scope, but—on the contrary—the fact that the city was now trying to curb expansion. For decade after decade, priority had been given to industrial growth, and especially to heavy industry. With industrial growth the population had swelled. Muscovites once gloried in the city's increasing size, even though it was bought at the expense of crowding and overtaxed facilities. Now, the mayor talked of cutting down the level of heavy industry, preventing any further large-scale population influx, solving the housing problem and improving services.

This shift in emphasis, even in plans still largely on paper, seemed almost revolutionary. In a Moscow still hard-pressed by shortages, the mayor held forth a vision of quality of life as a major objective. In a city infatuated with the automobile, he said he was pleading with the central government to sell fewer cars in Moscow: "Sell them in the villages, I told them. I have seen the Paris traffic problem. We don't want it."

It was refreshing to hear this—indeed, it was breath-taking in the Moscow setting—but, just as foreigners in the 1930s wondered whether Moscow could build its new industries, so I wondered whether it could stop its headlong growth.

The specific new Moscow plan will run to 1985; broad guidelines are projected to the year 2000. The crucial point in the plan, in the eyes of most Muscovites, is more and better housing. Since the 1950s Moscow has set records in its mass production of prefabricated units. The mayor boasted that already more than 70 per cent of Moscow's current housing had been built since 1945. To the foreign visitor, the long avenues of monotonous blocks may be a depressing sight, but to Muscovites they are a gleaming promise that some day Moscow will close the last communal flat and give each family separate housing and each person a room. Meantime, the architectural monotony is being relieved by trees and

A gilded statue of a woman at Moscow's permanent Exhibition of National Economic Achievements represents the Soviet Republic of Georgia. In her hands she holds grapes and a sprig of tea, two of Georgia's main crops.

greenery, by variations in the lay-outs, and by improvements on the crude materials used in the 1950s and 1960s.

Moscow's builders are erecting standardized neighbourhoods ("micro-boroughs", they call them), each of which houses about 20,000 persons. During the 1950s and 1960s they were so intent on producing housing that often they left the schools, shops, clinics, nurseries, kindergartens and cafeterias to the last—sometimes with delays of years, to the anguish of residents. During the 1970s they corrected matters, and by the mid-1970s they were constructing an experimental neighbourhood, Chertanovo, with such modern improvements as underground street traffic, air conditioning (a novelty in Moscow housing), indoor swimming pools and gymnasiums, rubbish collection via vacuum tubes and compression of the rubbish to a tenth of its original volume to make removal easier. Chertanovo is intended as a model for the future Moscow.

After housing, priority goes to the need for services and shopping facilities. The trouble on this score is a shortage of labour. Most of the employees of the factories that were moved out of town in 1975 remained in the city, but, the mayor reported, Moscow was nevertheless short by at least 150,000 workers of the number the city required. "It is harder to find unskilled labour than specialists," he said, "harder to find nurses than doctors. We are planning to build thousands of new retail shops. We need shop clerks." The solution, he thought, was to modernize industry, introduce more self-service shops, reduce labour needs rather than import more labour.

Early in the 1970s the Russian Republic Ministry of Services to the Public called upon Moscow to improve service and repair enterprises, and to recruit pensioners, housewives and invalids to staff them. Magazines have begun to print pictures of waiters, cooks and hairdressers alongside those of honoured bricklayers and lathe operators. A magazine for young people hailed a truck driver for becoming a waiter in spite of the chiding of family and friends, who felt he was demeaning himself. Such trades as hairdressing have been given new prestige. The barber whom I patronized, formerly a construction worker, attended school for a year, then served an apprenticeship in a barber shop, and finally, in 1970, came to the city's most fashionable unisex salon, the Charodeika (Sorceress), which employs 150 hairdressers. He has become a "master, international class" in his trade and has trained the national men's hairdressing team for competitions among Communist countries. The walls of the Charodeika director's office hold a 1970 medal won in Paris and pennants from Polish and Argentine hair styling contests—quite a step up from the usual neighbourhood hairdresser's shop, and a new note in proletarian Moscow.

After the need for services, in the estimation of many Muscovites, and well ahead of most needs, city authorities agree, comes the battle against environmental pollution. By 1975 Moscow had converted the power

Frozen in flight, a sculpted rocket rides a soaring plume of titanium 328 feet high in one of Moscow's most striking modern monuments: the Space Exploration Obelisk. Built in 1964 to commemorate Soviet space achievements, the obelisk is displayed outside the Exhibition of National Economic Achievements.

for industrial and municipal plants from oil and coal to gas, built dust and gas purification installations at 780 industrial enterprises, shut down more than 300 enterprises deemed unhealthy, ordered others rebuilt to official sanitary standards, and by stringent control of effluent treatment restored fishing in the Moscow River in the centre of town. Moscow claims world records among large cities for being smoke-free and free of carbon monoxide fumes, but the lower Moscow River (inside the city, but beyond the centre) and some of its tributaries remain polluted. A decision has been taken to convert all buses to natural gas, although it may be many years before the decision is put into effect.

If Moscow is to cut down on its industrial concentration, where are the factories to go? To a ring of 14 satellite towns that will be built beyond the green belt that encircles Moscow. They will be satellite towns, the mayor emphasized, not commuter suburbs; his goal was to reduce the daily commuter flow of 500,000 by about half. To cut down on the traffic jams that have already begun to beset the city, he planned to double the length of Metro lines within the city to about 210 miles by 1985, and add another 65 miles by the year 2000. There would also be two more concentric ring roads within the existing rings of the city by 1985. Underground roadways, underground parking places, underground shopping malls and underground warehouses are also to be built. In addition, the overall long range plan provides for moving more people to the outskirts of the city—the part of town that used to be the slums in every Russian city but is now a desired area of superior housing. Moscow is to be divided into eight more or less self-sufficient zones, each with its own shops, theatres, and employment close to home. An experimental plant to convert rubbish to fertilizer is to be enlarged and several additional plants built.

One essential factor in this whole concept is prevention of a population influx. Twice before, Moscow plans have set restrictions on growth of population, and twice before the restrictions proved futile. The new Year 2000 plan is designed to hold the population stable at 8,000,000. What makes this goal more feasible than previous goals of 5,000,000 and 6,000,000 is the programme of diverting heavy industry to the satellite towns, while concentrating on the expansion of sophisticated precision industrial projects, such as in the field of electronics, which call for a skilled but relatively small workforce. Whether the city can hold back the population influx nevertheless is questionable.

Between the satellite towns and the city a 30-mile wide ring of parkland is to form a recreation zone. Having wrested control of housing from industry which in the past built and operated part of it, Moscow is now engaged in a struggle to wrest from the province the control of this leisure area. The need is acute, for the city is short of holiday recreational facilities for adults—hotels, sanatoriums, camp grounds and shelters for hikers.

Moscow's children fare better; three-quarters of them can go to summer camp for 26 days, but the children's summer holiday is about 70 days long. Very few holiday facilities are provided for entire families, which serves to explain why one-quarter of Moscow families have either built their own private summer cottages or rent rooms in the summer from outlying farmers. The *dacha* zone has been filling up at an alarming rate; construction costs have risen, and the pressure to permit the building of more private *dachas* has continued to mount. However, if the city can acquire control over the 30-mile "recreation zone" around it, presumably Moscow will be able to stem the haphazard private building and erect the communal leisure facilities its citizens are now short of.

Above all, the city administrators have the eternal problem of coping with shortages. The city may reap a profit from its various enterprises and have no difficulty in funding services and construction, but all of the roubles in the U.S.S.R. cannot buy all of the materials, labour and equipment needed—sometimes not even all the food the city wants. A budget surplus sounds enticing to a Western mayor, but in Moscow it may signify that funds simply could not be fully expended because supplies and manpower were in short supply. The mayor and his aides battle against such problems constantly and fight their way through the bureaucratic tangles of central, republic and local agencies for the sake of "the plan"—this time a new plan to improve the quality of life.

Now, finally, I wonder, is Moscow really going to slow down the explosive growth that began more than 100 years ago when the serfs were emancipated? Is it going to enjoy a long-postponed relaxation and put badly needed finishing touches on the raw city? Or will Moscow's managers find the city still running hard merely to catch up?

Moscow is still a boom town. Traffic roars down the 12-lane avenues. Wrecking crews are ripping out rows of buildings to create more avenues. Construction cranes stand everywhere against the sky. New streets stretch for miles.

All the changes are scheduled to be completed in the year 2000. Will it all work out? I can only offer the same response that the confident young Moscow students gave me in the 1930s when I asked them if the ambitious industrialisation plans would succeed: Wait.

Lazy, Golden Days of Summer

PHOTOGRAPHS BY PETE TURNER

On a bank of the Moscow River an angler bends over his gear. For a small girl, however, running after paper aeroplanes is much more absorbing than fishing.

Muscovites, many of whom grew up in the country, have a passion for the outdoors. Those who dwell in crowded apartments would find life unbearable—especially in summer—were it not for the city's abundance of open space. Moscow has some 26 wooded parks, several of them with easy access to the Moscow River. Patches of undisturbed forest can also be found in the midst of high-rise housing estates, and the official plan for Moscow's growth ensures that more such areas will be preserved. In addition, a short bus or train ride takes Muscovites into a countryside uncluttered by the kind of suburban development that surrounds many Western cities. On hot days hundreds of thousands go to the country or the parks. They picnic, swim, play games, drink *kvas* (Russian rye beer) or simply bare their white limbs to the summer sun.

On an early summer day, when the air is hot but the Moscow River remains too cold for swimming, women hitch up their skirts to wade in the shallows.

Within sight of the tall cranes that exemplify the city's high-rise building boom, Muscovites still find space to sun themselves on the river's grassy shore.

A swimmer, who knows the water is deeper than it looks, plunges into a pond in Vorontsovo Park, once the estate of a Russian noble family. In spite of its rustic appearance, the park is well inside the city limits of Moscow.

Yellow-tinged leaves in Vorontsovo Park signal the end of summer, but the foliage is still thick enough to enhance the pleasant solitude of a Moscow woman strolling on her own, away from her overcrowded home.

Bibliography

Baedeker, Karl B., *Baedeker's Russia, 1914.* Allen & Unwin and David & Charles, Newton Abbot, London, 1971.

Balanenko, Yuri and Berezin, Alexander, *My Capital—My Moscow.* Izdatelstvo Planeta, Moscow, 1974.

Bortoli, Georges, *Moscow and Leningrad Observed.* Translated by Amanda and Edward Thompson. Kaye & Ward, London, 1975.

Dvinsky, Emilian, *Moscow from A to Y.* (In Russian.) Moskovsky Rabochy, Moscow, 1969.

Dvoinov, V., *Moscow in Questions and Answers.* (In Russian.) Moskovsky Rabochy, Moscow, 1973.

Fedosyuk, Yuri, *The Boulevard Ring.* (In Russian.) Moskovsky Rabochy, Moscow, 1972.

Fisher, Lynn and Wesley, *The Moscow Gourmet—Dining Out in Moscow.* Ardis, Ann Arbor, Michigan, 1974.

Floyd, David, *Russia in Revolt—1905: The First Crack in Tsarist Power.* Macdonald & Co., London, 1969.

Girard, Marcel and George, Pierre, *Nagels Encyclopedia Guide—Moscow and its Environs.* Nagel, Geneva, 1973.

Gray, Camilla, *The Russian Experiment in Art 1863-1922.* Thames and Hudson, London, 1962.

Gilyarovsky, Vladimir, *Moscow and the Muscovites.* (In Russian.) Moskovsky Rabochy, Moscow, 1968.

Grishin, Viktor V., *Speech at the 24th Communist Party Congress,* in *Current Soviet Policies VI.* American Slavic Studies Association, Columbus, Ohio, 1973.

Gunther, John, *Inside Russia Today.* Hamish Hamilton, London, 1958.

Ilyin, Mikhail A., *Moscow—Architecture and Monuments.* Progress, Moscow, 1968.

Ilyin, Mikhail A., *Moscow—Monuments of Architecture of the 18th and First Third of the 19th Century (2 vols.).* (In English and Russian.) Iskusstvo, Moscow, 1975.

Kaiser, Robert G., *Russia—The People and the Power.* Secker & Warburg, London, 1976.

Katkov, George and Shukman, Harold, *Lenin's Path to Power—Bolshevism and the Destiny of Russia.* Macdonald, London, 1971.

Khomov, S. S. (ed.), *History of Moscow.* (In Russian.) Nauka, Moscow, 1974.

Miller, Arthur, *In Russia.* Secker & Warburg, London, 1969.

Mishchenko, Alexei, *Memorable Places in Moscow.* (In Russian.) Reklama, Moscow, 1973.

Myachin, Ivan, *Moscow.* (In Russian.) Moskovsky Rabochy, Moscow, 1973.

Myachin, Ivan and Chernov, Vladimir, *Moscow Tourist Guide.* Novosti Press Agency Publishing House, Moscow, 1967.

Newman, Bernard, *To Russia and Back.* Barrie & Jenkins, London, 1967.

Pares, Bernard, *A History of Russia.* Knopf, New York, 1947.

Posokhin, M. V., *Cities to Live In.* Novosti Press Agency Publishing House, Moscow, 1974.

Promyslov, Vladimir F., *Speech at the 23rd Communist Party Congress,* in *Current Soviet Policies V.* American Slavic Studies Association, Columbus, Ohio, 1973.

Rubinov, A., *The City Fathers.* (In Russian.) Moskovsky Rabochy, Moscow, 1966.

Salisbury, Harrison E., (ed.), *The Soviet Union—The Fifty Years.* Brace & World, New York, 1967.

Schecter, Leona and Jerrold, *An American Family in Moscow.* Little, Brown & Co., Boston/Toronto, 1975.

Shvidkovsky, O. A., (ed.), *Building in the U.S.S.R. 1917-1932.* Studio Vista, London, 1971.

Smith, Hedrick, *The Russians.* Times Books, London, 1976.

Soloukhin, Vladimir A., *Letters from the Russian Museum.* (In Russian.) Sovetskaya Rossia, Moscow, 1967.

Sytin, P. V., *History of the Planning and Building of Moscow (3 vols.).* (In Russian.) Museum of History of Moscow, Moscow, 1953-1972.

Taubman, William, *Governing Soviet Cities—Bureaucratic Politics and Urban Development in the U.S.S.R.* Praeger, New York, 1973.

Tarsis, Valeriy, *Russia and the Russians.* Macdonald, London, 1970.

Trofimov, Vladimir, *Moscow, Borough by Borough.* (In Russian.) Moskovsky Rabochy, Moscow, 1972.

Troyat, Henri, *Daily Life in Russia under the Last Tsar.* Allen & Unwin, London, 1961.

Veselkovsky, S., *The Moscow Region—Memorable Places in the History of Russian Culture from the 14th to the 19th Century.* (In Russian.) Moskovsky Rabochy, Moscow, 1955.

Voyce, Arthur, *The Moscow Kremlin—Its History, Architecture and Art Treasures.* Greenwood Press, Westport, Conn., 1954.

Werth, Alexander, *Russia at War, 1941-1945.* Barrie & Jenkins, London, 1964.

Acknowledgements and Picture Credits

The author and editors wish to thank the following for their valuable assistance:

Tony Allan, London; Charles Dettmer, Thames Ditton, Surrey; Susan Goldblatt, London; Intourist, London; Norman Kolpas, London; Mark Krupkin, Novosti Press Agency, Moscow; Lornie Leete-Hodge, Devizes, Wiltshire; Museum of the History and Reconstruction of Moscow, Moscow; Theodore Shabad, New York; John Shaw, Melbourne; Ludmilla Smirnova, VAAP, Soviet Copyright Agency, Moscow; Society for Cultural Relations with the U.S.S.R., London.

Sources for pictures in this book are shown below, with the exception of those already credited. Credits for pictures from left to right are separated by commas: from top to bottom by dashes.

Cover, front end paper, 4—Pete Turner. 6, 7—Dick Rowan. 8, 9—Mr. Rakhmanov, Moscow—(insert) from the John Hillelson Collection. 10, 11—Pete Turner. 12, 13—Map by Hunting Surveys Ltd., London. Silhouettes by Anna Pugh. 17, 22, 23—Pete Turner. 24—Dick Rowan. 25—(top) Dick Rowan, Claudia Rowan, Farrell Grehan—(middle) Dick Rowan, Pete Turner, Dick Rowan—(bottom) Dick Rowan. 26—Pete Turner. 27—Anthony Edgeworth. 28, 29—Pete Turner. 30, 31—Farrell Grehan. 37—(top right-middle centre) Dick Rowan. 40, 41—Novosti Press Agency. 43—Popperfoto. 46, 47, 49, 52, 53, 72, 73—Pete Turner. 76, 77, 79, 96 to 99, 122, 123, 127, 131—Dick Rowan. 133—Farrell Grehan. 135—Dick Rowan—Farrell Grehan. 138, 139—Dick Rowan. 140, 142, 143—Pete Turner. 144—Dick Rowan. 145—Farrell Grehan. 146 to 148—Pete Turner. 152—Dick Rowan. 153, 155, 158, 159, 163—Pete Turner. 178—Farrell Grehan. 182, 183, 185—Pete Turner. 187—Dick Rowan.

Index

Numerals in italics indicate a photograph or drawing of the subject mentioned

Colour reproduction by Irwin Photography Ltd., at their Leeds PDI Scanner Studio.
Filmsetting by C. E. Dawkins (Typesetters) Ltd., London, SE1 1UN.
Printed and bound in Italy by Arnoldo Mondadori, Verona.